A Christian Environmentalist

An Oxymoron or an Obligation?

By

E. Roberts Alley

Copyright © 2013 by E. Roberts Alley

A Christian Environmentalist
An Oxymoron or an Obligation?
by E. Roberts Alley

Printed in the United States of America

ISBN 9781626972759

All rights reserved solely by the author. The author guarantees all contents are original and do not infringe upon the legal rights of any other person or work. No part of this book may be reproduced in any form without the permission of the author. The views expressed in this book are not necessarily those of the publisher.

Unless otherwise indicated, Bible quotations are taken from The English Standard Version of the Bible. Copyright © 2001 by Crossway Bibles; and The New American Standard Bible. Copyright © 1971 by The Lockman Foundation

www.xulonpress.com

Table of Contents

Preface xvii
Chapter 1 - The Players in the Green
    Game 21
    The Environmentalist 22
    The Protesters 25
    The Polluters 27
    The Conservatives 28
    The Christians 29
    Can the Green Players
    Communicate with each Other 30
Chapter 2 - Do We Accept the Supernatural? 32
    The Holy Spirit and the Supernatural 36
    Natural or Supernatural Creation? 38
Chapter 3 - Our Communication with
    the Supernatural 40
    Our Brain and Heart 40
    Our Genetic Nature 42
    Our Soul 43
    Our Spirit 45
    Our Mind 45

Our God 46
What Does This Mean? 47
The Existence of God 47
The Truth of the Bible 48
Bible Translations 53
The Rest of the Book 54
Chapter 4 - The Environment Today 55
Pollution of the Environment 57
Air Pollution 60
Greenhouse Gases 63
Global Warming 66
Climate Change 68
Water Pollution 69
Land Pollution 73
Hydraulic Fracturing 75
Regulatory Trends 76
Chapter 5 - God Speaks Out About the
  Environment through Creation 81
Organics and Inorganics 83
Day One of Creation, The Earth 85
Day Two of Creation, the Sky 88
Day Three of Creation, Vegetation 88
Day Four of Creation,
  the Universe and Time 91
Day Five of Creation,
  Aquatic Life and Birds 96
Day Six of Creation,
  Animals and man 97
Chapter 6 - God's Purpose
  for Mankind 99
Dust and God's Breath 99
Man's Service to the Environment 102

Table of Contents

    The Difference is Blood 105
Chapter 7 - The Rise, Fall and Re-Creation
    of the Environment 107
    The Rise and Fall of the Old World 107
    The Re-Creation of the New World 109
    The Need for a New World 109
    Our Environment in the New World 113
    No More Death 115
    The New Heaven and the New Earth.............115
    The Survival of Organics and Inorganics 116
Chapter 8 - Science Speaks Out
    About the Environment...................................119
    Science and Engineering are Different 122
    The Limitations of Science 123
    Our Challenge to Clean up the air..................127
    Air Source Testing 128
    Air Emissions Testing 128
    Air Pollutants 129
    Air Pollution Control Methods 131
    Carbon Dioxide Control.................................133
    Air Regulatory Compliance 144
    Our Challenge to Clean up the Water 137
    Physical Treatment of Wastewater 138
    Chemical Treatment of Wastewater 140
    Biological Treatment of Wastewater 143
    Our Challenge to Clean up the Land...............144
Chapter 9 - Our Stewardship of
    the Environment...146
    Will I be a Christian Environmentalist?.........146
    Preserving our Bodies and our Minds............148
    Available Natural Resources 150
    Air Resources...150

Water Resources 151
Land Resources 151
The Residuals of Civilization 152
Natural Residuals 152
Agricultural Residuals 153
Municipal Residuals 153
Industrial Residuals 153
Personal Residuals 154
What We Can Do 155
Residuals Accounting 156
The Mission Statement 157
Plan Boundary 157
Geographical Boundary 158
Organizational Boundary 158
Life Cycle Analysis 158
Estimating Residual Discharges 159
Calculations for Direct Discharges 160
Calculations for Indirect Discharges 161
Estimating Transportation Discharges 162
Other Discharges 163
What Then? 163
Practical Examples 164
Why is it Important? 166
Why We are Here 167
About the Author 169
Books by E. Roberts Alley 171

Dedication

This book is dedicated to Jesus Christ and the other most important people of my life: my late wife, Marion; our children: Rob, Lea, Aime and Emma; their spouses: Fronda, Steve, Scott and Jeff; and their children: Reagan, Hayes, Grace and Otis; Will and Cooper; Catherine and Wesley; and Jimmy. I love you all!

Acknowledgements

I must first give thanks to my late wife Marion who encouraged me and proof read manuscript after manuscript and hopefully made the book more readable. My children listed in the Dedication have also helped me to edit as did Larry Stone, Author; Norman Rohrer, Author; Scotty Smith, Author and Pastor; Richard Jennings, Pastor; Frank Sizemore, Industrial Director of Regulatory Affairs; John S. Coulter P.E., Consulting Environmental Engineer; E. Roberts Alley, Jr., P.E., Consulting Engineer; and Richard E. Speece, Author and Centennial Professor of Civil and Environmental Engineering Emeritus, Vanderbilt University.

Academically. Professors Wesley Eckenfelder, Edward Thackston and George Malaney at Vanderbilt University Graduate School taught me that Environmental Engineering is a science consisting of multiple disciplines that can solve most of our environmental challenges.

Theologically, I am indebted to many Christian teachers over the years including Pastors Cortez Cooper, Scotty Smith, Richard Jennings, Ray Ortlund, Jim Bachmann and Dustin Sedlak.

Above all, I am submitted to my Lord and Savior, Jesus Christ who loves me unconditionally and has held my hand during the writing of this book.

Endorsements

"In Bob Alley's latest book, *A Christian Environmentalist*, readers are able to reap from his unique perspective as a long term student of science <u>and</u> Scripture. He fills a niche which provides keen insight into the subject of environmentalism. Hopefully the door will be opened for many like minded professionals to follow." Richard Jennings, Pastor

"In his new book, *A Christian Environmentalist*, Bob Alley not only demonstrates the compatibility of faith and science, he also demonstrates the beautiful relationship between the gospel of grace and the stewardship of God's world. As Bob clearly demonstrates, followers of Jesus should be those who enjoy God's creation to the fullest, and those involved in environmental issues- including exploring, cultivating and protecting the earth." Scotty Smith, Pastor

"Mr. Alley has struck an important public nerve with his call for an honest look at the neo-pagan aspects of portions of the environmental movement.

He has the credentials to present the scientific details while remaining true to both the Biblical mandate and responsibility. Christians have to subdue and guard the earth until Christ's return. *A Christian Environmentalist* should not be overlooked by anyone wishing to be aware of the environmental and political issues confronting us." W.Z. Baumgartner, Jr. P.E., CHMM, REM, DEE, W.Z. Baumgartner & Assoc, Inc., Environmental Engineers & Consultants

"Mr. E. Roberts Alley is one of the best environmental engineers that I have ever had the pleasure to know and work with. His knowledge of environmental science and his ability to apply his engineering skills to solve complex environmental problems are second to none. He is also one of the few individuals I have known that applies his Christian beliefs to every facet of his life, including his professional career as an engineer and entrepreneur. In his book, *A Christian Environmentalist, An Oxymoron or an Obligation,* Mr. Alley provides an excellent study in the fundamentals of environmental science and man's impact on the environment, along with a very sound Biblical foundation on man's responsibility toward the environment. The study concludes with some very basic understandable guidelines on why it's important for Christians to be environmentalists along with some practical steps on how to be a better environmentalist. I would highly recommend this book for anyone who has any concerns about the environment and where their responsibilities lie." John S. Coulter, P.E., Coulter Engineering Services

Endorsements

"I've known Bob Alley as a successful environmental engineer and as a committed Christian for almost 40 years. He is eminently qualified to write an environmental guidebook like *The Christian Environmentalist*. Bob has accomplished a very difficult task in making this book technically sound, consistent with the teaching of the Bible, and a very interesting read. This is a timely book and I will be recommending it to many friends". Michael Tant P.E., Consulting Engineer.

"I have known Bob Alley for almost 15 years, mostly as a client in his environmental consulting business. Bob has always provided me with sound environmental engineering that has allowed me to complete critical air and water pollution prevention projects in the industrial manufacturing arena. In recent years Bob and I have had the opportunity to share our faith with each other and how that faith in the Creator God works out in the three dimensional world that we live and work in. Bob's astute engineering mind and the depth of his Bible knowledge provide a cogent and unique incite to what environmental stewardship is really about. Thank you Bob for allowing the Lord to "will and act in you according to His good purpose". Frank Sizemore- Certified Hazardous Materials Manager, Director of Regulatory Affairs, Chemical Manufacturing

"The author is a strong writer; the style of writing is articulate and intelligent, yet still conversational. The author's knowledge of the subject matter is more like expertise, and the depth and scope of this very comprehensive manuscript is a reflection of that. The author does an excellent job, however, of breaking the material down for the reader so that it is understandable. The author provides an ample amount of research and scripture to back up each of the points which he raises. The reader will be able to clearly see the scientific and biblical basis for the premises which are presented." Editorial Department, Xulon Press

Preface

I love the outdoors! I love good, clean air, crystal clear streams, and animals and plants in the wild. All Christians who love God should love the environment He created for us to enjoy. Each of us has a responsibility to examine our relation to its care and keeping.

Since God created our environment, do we have the right or the freedom to allow His "good" creation to deteriorate? Are we truly stewards of the environment with dominion over it and a responsibility to protect it from damage and to enhance its usefulness?

What is our responsibility to the environment? Do we even have one? Since the late 19th century with Gifford Pinchot and John Muir, the *book ends* in this discussion have polarized even more to: ignore nature in our fight for survival and growth (abuse); and return nature to its original state with no evidence of man's existence (worship).

This book addresses each issue from a Christian perspective. God summons us to rule over nature and subdue it, and promises to provide the wisdom and means to follow His commands.

Have you stood on a mountain top under the spell of the splendor and beauty, or sat on the sea shore and wondered how God can put the colors of a rainbow or sunset together in a way not approached in our best art? Have you looked at a wild animal or bird and marveled at the perfection of its beauty and functionality? Studying an oak tree, a snowflake, a desert flower or a mossy knoll can cause us to feel the joy of standing in our free art gallery called nature. If you have had any of these experiences, you would certainly want to bequeath them to the next generations.

Imagine a world as pure as the one which God first created. That will be true in Heaven, but because of the Fall, the quest for a pure environment cannot be realized until the consummation. Therefore, our goal on this earth is to maintain a sustainable environment, one in which humans can co-exist with, and enjoy natural vegetation and animals, while allowing population and the industries and jobs that serve population, to grow.

We are told in Genesis 1:28 to: *Be fruitful and multiply; fill the earth and subdue it*. This command of God to subdue the earth, is followed in the same verse with the answer to the difficult position in which God has placed us: *and have dominion over the fish of the sea and over the birds of the heavens and over every living thing that moves on the earth*. Indeed, we can subdue the earth, since we have the power of supreme authority over all living things.

Preface

The purpose of this book is to explore these commands of God, which are contradictory in the eyes of the non-believing world, to see how both the Bible and science have given us this opportunity and challenge.

As author of this book, I feel comfortable speaking to scientific issues as a teacher, a scientist and a Professional Engineer with many years experience in teaching and helping industries and municipalities to treat their waste products so they will not negatively affect the environment. I speak to the mandates of the Bible with only the humble confidence expressed in 1 Peter 4:11: *whoever speaks, as one who speaks oracles of God; whoever serves as one who serves by the strength that God supplies- in order that in everything God may be glorified through Jesus Christ. to* Him *belong glory and dominion forever and ever. Amen.* I am especially humbled since I came from being a theistic evolutionist with very private and liberal Christian beliefs, to a theistic Trinitarian view of God, and an infallible and inerrant view of the Scriptures. In this book, I quote God from Scripture much more often than I do the writings of natural man, because God in His perfect communication, is the only One truly knowledgeable about this subject.

I have spent 60 years studying the two passions of my life, God's Word and the environment, and have written this book to pass on some of my conclusions from this study. I write to communicate to anyone who is seriously interested in reaching closer to the truth in these two areas, whether they be Christians or not, theologians, preachers or religious workers;

environmentalists, environmental professionals or interested lay people. I warn you that no writing of man can communicate the complete truth of the Bible or of the environment, only God through the Bible itself can do this. So my goal is to lead you to critically think about these issues, question your beliefs and the beliefs of others, and open yourself up to what God is communicating to you about your life and your relation to the environment. In Ecclesiastes 8:17, Solomon says: *then I saw all the works of God, that man cannot find out the work that is done under the sun. However much man may toil in seeking, he will not find it out. Even though a wise man claims to know, he cannot find it out.*

This book is organized into a discussion about the environmental controversy, the question of the supernatural, a description of today's environmental condition, what God says about the environment, what science says about the environment, and how we can be stewards of the environment.

All references except for brief ones are shown as footnotes to the text, rather than at the end of the chapter, to make them more available. Facts quoted without a reference are either from the author's knowledge or readily available on the internet.

Chapter 1

The Players in the Green Game

y first serious encounter with the environment was in meeting the requirements of the Nature Merit Badge on the way to becoming an Eagle Scout. I suppose as a young *pre-engineer* type boy, I was more interested in the exciting merit badges such as Pioneering, Camping and Canoeing. But I had to pass Nature, and one of the requirements was to find a place in the woods, spend what seemed to me an eternity at that spot, and write a paper on my experience.

To put it mildly, I was blown away by being quietly immersed in nature. To sit in complete silence in the middle of a forest and observe the beauty of the vegetation, the excitement of seeing animals and birds up close, changed my entire perspective on the environment. Instead of a Civil, Structural or

Mechanical Engineer, I became an Environmental Engineer.

Every person is forced sooner or later, to have an intimate relation to the environment. That often abused word encompasses all air, water, and land spheres of our planet (and beyond), and includes all living creatures therein. The environment is really nature; in other words, everything that exists naturally. We exist within this framework, and depending upon our stewardship, we may live in concert with nature, or we may suffer severe consequences due to our neglect and abuse of nature.

The Environmentalist

Does our dependence on the environment give us an obligation to protect the environment, or as a pervasive force, should we fear, or even worship it? Our society sometimes seems to be composed of those who abuse nature, assuming that it will heal itself, or those who worship nature as god. The majority of us choose to enjoy the beauty of nature and expend at least a minimum effort toward preserving that beauty. But what of the more passionate environmentalists who feel and/or fear that the existence and practices of the human portion of the environment are destroying the very integrity of nature; and that nature will not exist in the near future as it does today?

We have read that one of the more extreme environmental zealots, when asked the ideal population of the earth, answered *zero* (Earth First founder David Foreman). In other words, he believes that the waste products created by mankind, unlike those created by animals or plants, have a negative and permanent effect on nature by definition. Foreman, in his *Confessions of an Eco-Warrior* said *An individual human life has no more intrinsic value than does an individual grizzly life,* and *A placing of earth first in all decisions, even ahead of human welfare, is necessary.* He has consistently promoted environmental terrorism from his 1987 *A Field Guide to Monkey Wrenching* (spiking trees to injure loggers), to his quote in the May 1996 issue of *Nation, The blood of timber executives is my natural drink, and the wail of dying forest supervisors is music to my ears.*

More subtly, I first realized that many environmentalists have a goal of protecting their favorite parts of the environment for their own enjoyment and that of the *initiated*, rather than to let the unclean masses enjoy God's Creation. As a Scoutmaster, I had led part of my troop for three hours through an intricate cave system to show them the 1812 Passage, which was uncovered by a friend of mine for the first time since 1812, when I was in the cave. At that time the most recent date in the passage was 1812, as indicated by a torch marking on the cave wall. These Scouts had the opportunity to be among the first handful of people to visit this passage since it was sealed. When we arrived at the end of the passage, I showed them my name along with the names of a couple of my friends who were in the cave on that memorable day when it was first re-opened. Much to my disappointment, our names and dates were crossed out by subsequent visitors. Obviously these exclusive spelunkers felt that we had desecrated the cave, but the names of the 1812 explorers were preserved. I think that this is a good example of the subtle desire to restrict nature to the *natural* part of nature and miss the important point that mankind is very much a part of nature as the culmination of His Creation. As such, man's visits to nature can be described on site in a dignified way in order to document the history of that part of nature. Without that freedom, we would not have known that the passage had been sealed since 1812, or the names and dates of the Confederate soldiers who mined saltpeter in another portion of this same cave system. Most environmentalists sadly, seem to overlook the fact that humans are part of nature, and exacerbate their mistake by trying to limit the association of the public with nature to those who, in their judgment, will preserve nature in a way that will not reveal mankind's ever having been there. Other examples are the attempts by environmentalists to prevent roadways through parks (I 40 through Overton Park in Memphis, TN), the prevention of the Keystone Pipeline from Canada to Texas because of environmental concerns, the prevention of flood control dams in order to protect the endangered snail darter, and the loss of billions of dollars caused by the stoppage of nuclear power plants after construction was well on its way.

We hear daily of dire warnings of global cooling, global warming, climate change and animal and vegetative species destruction which are caused by the actions of humans. These passionate voices have an effect on environmental legislation and the cost of living for each of us, even without credible scientific reasoning.

The voices on both sides of this issue bring up legitimate questions which we should consider and address. Is sustainable development of the human race possible at our present structure of taxation? If not, we may need to pay more for goods and/or increase our taxes in order to improve the environment. Can we, or should we, re-distribute the expenditures of our governments to allocate a higher percentage to environmental protection?

Some feel that the money now spent for this purpose is the result of the efforts of a few misguided environmentalists who want to preserve nature as it is, or as it used to be, in order for them to enjoy it privately as *initiates* who are especially qualified to respect and protect the sensitivity of nature. Does all nature exist for the benefit and enjoyment of all people, or can parts of it only be trusted to experts?

It seems that politicians believe that the government owns the environment, land owners believe that they do, and Christians believe that God owns and has responsibility for nature. And they all believe that they are the real environmentalists.

The Protesters

When a citizen of the United States sees blatant abuse of the environment by industries, municipalities, businesses, or citizens, there are legal processes that can be taken to report and hopefully prevent this abuse. Many concerned citizens become frustrated at the lack of response to reports of environmental abuse and resort to public protests for results. Some of these protests are non-violent in the spirit of Dr. Martin Luther King, but others are deliberately violent in order, presumably to get quicker results.

Some legal protests have been carried out in the name of the environment, but actually have the hidden purpose of limiting growth or population increase for selfish purposes. I have seen repeatedly, newcomers to an attractive area trying to prevent others from having the same opportunity that they had, by opposing a new development. Even the science of Land Planning has been much abused for vested interests on both sides of the growth and urbanization controversy. Proper, fair and objective Land Planning is the reasonable answer.

I was visiting a client shortly after they had an unannounced *visit* by Greenpeace. The environmental group attacked the industry by trespassing on private property and climbing towers which contained pipes filled with chlorine gas, in order to mount a large sign announcing that this industry manufactured a certain chemical. The danger of this attack was minimized with the arrest of the protesters before any of the fragile chlorine lines were broken with resulting loss of life in the neighborhood. This *visit* followed the same Greenpeace group filling an industrial sewer manhole with concrete upstream of my client, resulting in the risk of causing an overflow of pollution into the Mississippi River. This organization, which is known for its Save the Whales campaign, has risked lives in Memphis as well as in other locations with these misguided antics.

Interviews of environmental protesters have shown that most participants are caught up in the excitement, emotion and romance of the protests, rather than understanding the issues and risks involved in their actions. These interviews are very similar to those of the recent o*ccupy protests*, more anti business than pro-environment, and tend to slow down the legitimate enforcement actions of the EPA and state regulatory departments.

The Polluters

On the other hand, we read of industries which display a blatant disregard for environmental issues and seek to maximize profits with the resulting pollution, leaving behind a dark trail of destruction. Their high priced legal expenses are considered a bargain compared to the cost of meeting environmental standards. We categorize politicians and political parties as being pro or anti environment, and may cast our votes accordingly.

Pollution is not always a selfish disregard of our responsibilities. Quite often, it can be the result of ignorance. For example, throwing trash out of a car window, smoking, and throwing paper on the ground are all acts of pollution. I have seen an industrial wastewater treatment system where toxic waste was put into a hole in the ground filled with limestone rocks. The owner bragged about the low capital cost of what he had constructed, unrealistically believing that the hazardous metals would be treated before entering the soil. I have also seen excavated holes on industrial sites into which streamed highly polluted groundwater, and have heard of many cases of buried drums of toxic chemicals.

My wife and I are avid Scuba divers and have seen the effect humans have on coral reefs and other aquatic life. We have seen trash, unnaturally broken coral, over fishing and the bleaching of coral by acidic waters.

The estuaries of rivers where they discharge into salt water, are especially sensitive to clear cutting, agriculture, and the runoff from cities and industries upstream.

So, each of us has been, or will be forced to address the question of our relationship to the environment and our response to some of these questions. Do we work within the law or violently protest to get results? Do we pollute personally while we protest publically, or do we just ignore pollution with the blind faith that it will heal itself?

The Conservatives

Conservatives and Republicans have recently denied all evidence of global warming and much environmental risk, by arguing that the need for jobs to provide recovery to the nation's economy, warrants the relaxation of environmental regulatory control. By doing this they are following the short term mentality of much liberal thinking and allowing the long term consequences to be passed on to a future generation. In effect, they are *throwing the baby out with the bathwater*, with the *bathwater* being the reasonable regulations and the *baby* being our future. Unfortunately, emotions, politics and panic tend to overwhelm good, long term scientific judgment in these cases. I speak further of this dilemma later in the book.

The Christians

Those of us who are Christians believe that God has communicated with us through His inspired Scriptures. The purpose of this book is to examine the scientific reality of the environment and the effect we as humans have on it from a Christian perspective. This analysis appears to be critical at this time because Christians are beginning to speak out, giving recommendations as to our mandate for protecting or freely using the environment. This interest, plus the daily media reports, make it necessary that we prepare ourselves with scientific and Biblical knowledge in order to take an intelligent and Christian position concerning our relation to the environment.

Can I, or should I be a Christian environmentalist, or is that an oxymoron, a conflict in terms? Those who call themselves Christians have argued passionately that we have an obligation to protect the environment from ourselves, while others of the same persuasion have argued that environmental protection by regulation is just a worship of nature as god.

The goal of this book is to study this question from a scientific perspective and from a Biblical perspective in order to determine a proper response of a Christian to the environment.

Can the Green Players Communicate with Each Other?

As we enter this study, we first should define the two key words of the question; *Christian* and *environmentalist*. Webster's Ninth New Collegiate Dictionary defines a Christian as *a follower of Christ*, and the environment as *surroundings; conditions of life or growth*. Therefore, according to these definitions, a Christian environmentalist is a follower of Christ who is concerned about their surroundings. This definition includes a very large percentage of people in the United States and even the world. So why are we so divided in our response to the environment and its protection?

As a Christian, is our responsibility to God, to nature, or to both, and what if those responsibilities conflict?

A potential answer is alluded to in Webster's second definition of the environment as *conditions of life or growth*. Webster, as most of us would, has limited the environment to our natural surroundings. But would a Christian consider that our surroundings are supernatural, or spiritual, as well as natural, or physical? Most non-religious people will limit their beliefs to the natural, since the natural can theoretically be proven by science. To them, science becomes a god, defining truth, and excluding from truth any thing, thought or feeling that is supernatural.

In contrast, Christian and non-Christian theologians, consistently believe in some level of the supernatural or spiritual. This belief cannot be proven, since it is beyond natural science, but it can be felt, be logically reasoned and can be reality as much as a fact of nature. In 2 Corinthians 45:18, Paul tells us: *as we look not to the things that are seen but to the things that are unseen. For the things that are seen are transient, but the things that are unseen are eternal.* Is God involved in our environment, or did He create it and let it be? Does He care about His creation, and if so, has He spoken to us of His interest and our mandate?

Chapter 2

Do We Accept the Supernatural?

This huge question of our acceptance of the supernatural must be answered if we are to truly understand reality, including the environment and science. The overwhelming majority of the population has some belief in the supernatural. It may be New Age, re-incarnation, mental telepathy, Hinduism, Buddhism, Muslim or Christian, but it is based on spirituality as reality. The ability to recognize that reality is not limited to natural occurrences, is one of the keys to understanding our relationship to the environment.

Many of us base our beliefs solely on the findings of science. This faith in the infallibility of science even extends to our interpretation of the Scriptures. The *Introduction to Genesis* in the *English Standard Version Study Bible*, asks and answers the question

Does Genesis 1 provide information in a way that corresponds to the purpose of modern science? To this question, the answer is no. The insinuation that God through Genesis had the responsibility of corresponding to the purposes of science, makes it clear that the question in the *Introduction* was misstated. Natural science is incapable of analyzing spiritual Creation, but a supernatural God is very much capable of speaking scientific truths, since He is the Creator of the natural world, and therefore, science.

If we believe in the supernatural, as Christians we must go to the Bible to find out the relationship between the natural and the supernatural. There is no other infallible source.

In John 3:12, Jesus says: *If I have told you earthly things and you do not believe, how can you believe if I tell you heavenly things?* Jesus is differentiating between earthly (natural) things, and heavenly (spiritual) things.

2 Corinthians 4:18 says: *as we look not to the things that are seen but to the things that are unseen. For the things that are seen are transient, but the things that are unseen are eternal.* Our real answers concerning our relation to the environment are in the unseen supernatural truths.

John 3:27 quotes John the Baptist as saying: *A person cannot receive even one thing unless it is given him from heaven.* John makes it clear that only spiritual things can really be received as important.

John 3:31 says: *He who comes from above is above all. He who is of the earth belongs to the earth and speaks in an earthly way. He who comes from*

Heaven is above all. This quote of John the Baptist tells us that he (as well as we) can only speak in an earthly way, but Jesus has seen and heard the spiritual truth, being God, and yet no one listens.

1 Corinthians 1:18 says: *For the Word of the Cross is folly to those who are perishing, but to us who are being saved it is the power of God. For it is written, 'I will destroy the wisdom of the wise, and the discernment of the discerning I will thwart'*. In this quote, Paul elaborates on the previous explanations by Jesus, John the Baptist and John the Apostle which speak of the natural and the supernatural. Paul makes the point that non believers have no capacity to understand spiritual truth, and consider it *folly*. He says in his quote from Isaiah 29:14, that their perceived wisdom and discerning will be destroyed.

1 Corinthians 2 says: *And I, when I came to you brothers, did not come to you proclaiming the testimony of God with lofty speech or wisdom. For I decided to know nothing among you except Jesus Christ and Him crucified. And I was with you in weakness and in fear and much trembling, and my speech and my message were not in plausible words of wisdom, but in demonstration of the Spirit and of power, that your faith might not rest in the wisdom of men but in the power of God. Yet upon the mature we do impart wisdom, although it is not a wisdom of this age or of the rulers of this age, who are doomed to pass away. But we impart a secret and hidden wisdom of God, which God decreed before the ages for our glory. None of the rulers of this age understood this, for if they had they would not*

have crucified the Lord of glory. But, as it is written, 'what no eye has seen, nor ear heard, nor the heart of man imagined, what God has prepared for those who love Him*'- these things God has revealed to us through the Spirit. For the Spirit searches everything, even the depths of God. For who knows a person's thoughts except the spirit of that person, which is in him? So also no one comprehends the Spirit of God. Now we have received not the spirit of the world but the Spirit who is from God, that we might understand the things freely given us by God. And we impart this in words not taught by human wisdom but taught by the Spirit, interpreting spiritual truths to those who are spiritual. The natural person does not accept the things of the Spirit of God, for they are folly to him, and he is not able to understand them because they are spiritually discerned. The spiritual person judges all things, but is himself to be judged by no one. 'For who has understood the mind of the Lord so as to instruct* Him*?' But we have the mind of Christ.* The highly educated author and speaker Paul, again in these verses, makes it very clear that he approached his ministry in weakness, fear and trembling and submitted his considerable gifts to God the Holy Spirit, the only interpreter of the eternal hidden wisdom of God. Paul understood that we his readers, as spiritual persons, also have the mind of Christ through the Holy Spirit, and can understand these spiritually discerned truths.

These verses, as well as many more, make it clear that natural science is not capable of giving us clear answers to spiritual questions. We must rely on the word of God. And as Christians, we must depend on our gift of the indwelling Holy Spirit for understanding and wisdom.

When we exclusively, through our efforts and intellect, attempt to discount or to explain the supernatural, we will become frustrated because the supernatural cannot be understood by the unregenerated natural mind. *We destroy arguments and every lofty opinion raised against the knowledge of God, and take every thought captive to obey Christ* (2 Corinthians 10:5). *At that time Jesus declared, 'I thank you Father, Lord of Heaven and earth, that You have hidden these things from the wise and understanding and revealed them to little children'* (Matthew 11:25).

Outside of many references to Creation, Jesus didn't speak much about natural science or even common sense. He didn't need to, for God has given mankind the intelligence to understand nature and apply common sense. Jesus' words were at a different level of reality, that of the spiritual world, which is not understandable through natural science or common sense. That is why we need the help of the Scriptures and the Holy Spirit to enable us to understand these mysteries

The Holy Spirit and the Supernatural

The Holy Spirit can allow us to understand the *hidden wisdom of God* (1Corinthians 2:7), and the *things freely given us by God* (in His Word) (1Corinthians 2:12). The Bible teaches that when we were saved by Jesus Christ through regeneration, we were filled with the Holy Spirit. Jesus left the Holy Spirit as part of the Trinity with us in His stead. Luke 24:49: *And behold, I am sending the promise of my Father upon you. But stay in the city until you are clothed with power from on high;* John 20:22: *And when He said this, He breathed on them and said to them 'Receive the Holy Spirit';* Acts 2:4: *And they were left all filled with the Holy Spirit.*

So that when we understand that we have no real power or understanding without God, we will receive the gift of the Holy Spirit, just like the Apostles and Disciples. When we receive that gift, we are regenerated as God's children with the inheritance of the disposition or life that was in Jesus (John 1:4: *In* Him *was life, and the life was the light of men;* John 8:12: *Again Jesus spoke to them saying 'I am the light of the world. Whoever follows* Me *will not walk in darkness, but will have the light of life';* John 12:46: *I have come into the world as light, so that whoever believes in* Me *may not remain in darkness.)*

That life that Jesus puts into us through the Holy Spirit when we are saved, enables us to discern between the natural and the supernatural and to see more clearly the revealed mysteries of God.

These mysteries will only become completely clear in Heaven but in this life, are sufficient for His purposes. Indeed, in Heaven, we will no longer have a need to understand, we will finally only be interested in God and His relation to us. Imagine how peaceful we will be then! 1 Corinthians 13:12 says: *For now we see in a mirror dimly, but then face to face. Now I know in part; then I shall know fully, even as I have been fully known.*

Natural or Supernatural Creation?

The Word of God teaches us that in the Creation, the supernatural is made natural: *as it is written, 'I have made you the father of many nations'- in the presence of the God in whom he believed, who gives life to the dead and calls into existence the things that do not exist*, (Romans 4:17 concerning the faith of Abraham).

This teaching allows us to understand the parallelism between the creation of the natural world from the supernatural existence of the Trinity, and the creation of the supernatural Christian saint from the natural man through Jesus Christ. *It is sown in dishonor; it is raised in glory. It is sown in weakness; it is raised in power It is sown a natural body; it is raised a spiritual body. If there is a natural body, there is also a spiritual body. Thus it is written, 'The first man Adam became a living being'; the last Adam became a life-giving spirit (I Corinthians 15: 43-45).*

The natural world, which was created from the supernatural, involves all things we sense. Colossians 1:16: *For by* Him *all things were created, in Heaven and in earth, visible and invisible, whether thrones or dominions or rulers or authorities- all things were created through* Him *and for* Him. So the purpose of this creation was through Jesus and for Jesus. Jesus therefore was the goal of Creation and therefore fully God.

Therefore, in order to completely understand the reality of the environment, and our responsibilities to the environment, we must understand that the environment was created by God supernaturally from that which did not exist, and will eventually return to the supernatural environment of Heaven (see Chapter 3).

This transcendence from supernatural to natural and back to supernatural can only be understood through the Creation by the triune God, the incarnation of God through Jesus Christ, and the resurrection of Jesus, His Saints and His environment, as allowed by His sacrifice, to break the curse on the environment caused by the original sin, the sin that we duplicate each time we want to be God.

We continue to reflect the weakness of Adam and Eve each time we taste of the tree of the knowledge of good and evil by claiming that we are as intelligent as God and can understand everything that He has done; and by claiming that we are as powerful as God and can control and fix the environment.

We can only understand what God allows us to understand. If we understand all that is in God's mind, we would be God, and pity the poor earth if that were so. So we can only control the damage we do to the environment, the understanding of which is the purpose of this book.

Chapter 3

Our Communication with the Supernatural

The Bible is consistent in differentiation between the natural and the supernatural aspects of the human, when it speaks of our heart, soul, spirit and mind, but there is obviously an interrelation between the terms. There has been discussion concerning these aspects from Plato, Augustine and Thomas Aquinas, and much is still being written.

Our Brain and Heart

Science has examined our brain and has some understanding of its function. After all, our brain is a physical organ which can be dissected and studied, but it is so complex that it has never been even partially reproduced outside of computer logic. We can live without the operation of parts of our brain due to damage, but we are said to be brain dead when our heart continues to pump, but our brain waves cease.

We speak of left brained people who are more mechanical and logical, and right brained people who are more creative and emotional. We even think that certain races or countries tend to produce left or right brained people. We know that the left and right sides of our brain control mechanical and creative functions, but we don't understand the reason that we are one or the other, except through heredity and/or the environment.

The Bible often is speaking of a combination of heart/brain functions when it uses the term *heart*. It is the seat of our emotions and involves cognitive and emotional responses. Matthew 6:21 says: *For where you treasure is, there your heart will be also.* Likewise Matthew 12:34: *You brood of vipers! How can you speak good when you are evil? For out of the abundance of the heart the mouth speaks.* Matthew 22:37: *And* He *said to him, 'You shall love the Lord your God with all your heart and with all your soul and with all your mind.*

This idea is also expressed in Deuteronomy 6:5: *You shall love the Lord your God with all your heart and with all your soul and with all your might.* See also Mark 12:30 (heart, soul, mind and strength), and Luke 10:27 (heart, soul, strength and mind) which express this "great commandment". Romans 10:10 says: *For with the heart one believes and is justified.* 1 Corinthians 4:5 says: *Therefore do not pronounce judgment before the time, before the Lord comes,* Who *will bring to light the things now hidden in darkness and will disclose the purposes of the heart.*

Revelation 2:23b says: *And all the churches will know that I am* He *who searches mind and heart, and I will give to each of you as your works deserve.*

Our Genetic Nature

One of the most fascinating natural parts of living organisms is that they all contain three major macromolecules, DNA, RNA and protein. In fact, this is one definition of life.

DNA (dioxyriboneucleic acid) carries the genetic information in the cell and is capable of self-replication and synthesis of RNA. DNA controls protein synthesis in cells and is the major constituent of the chromosomes within the cell nucleus. As such, DNA plays a central role in the determination of hereditary characteristics.

Plant DNA has the same chemical ingredients as animal DNA, but a different arrangement. RNA (ribonucleic acid) is involved in protein synthesis and the transmission of genetic information. These complex helix molecules consist of thousands of organic atoms which contain the programs which cause us to be plants or animals, humans or bacteria, dark or light pigmented, etc. Most of these molecules are inherited and allow scientists to prove ancestral relationships.

There is no creditable explanation for how these molecules have evolved from inorganic matter to have the capacity for programming organisms, and why DNA is so similar between species of plants and species of animals, and even between plants and animals. This is becoming more apparent as scientists continue to map the DNA of various species. Therefore, DNA logically appears to have been programmed by a supernatural intelligence which, unlike the god of nature, can plan, make decisions and control His Creation.

One of the interesting findings of DNA research is that programmed within these molecules is the ability for an organism to adapt to environmental change. It has become evident that natural selection as proposed by Darwin, is not contained in nature as evolution teaches, but in the organism itself.

Nature is not a single natural organism which can be broken down into molecules, but is a philosophical category containing matter, organic and inorganic; as a city contains buildings and people, bur cannot be tested without quantifying the structures and the population.

Our Soul

Webster's says that our soul is: *the material essence, animating principle, or activating cause of an individual life*. Psalms 19:7-8 says: *The law of the Lord is perfect, reviving the soul; the testimony of the Lord is sure, making wise the simple; the precepts of the Lord are right, rejoicing the heart; the commandment of the Lord is pure, enlightening the eyes*.

The Bible, many times, speaks of our soul as our spirit. Not the Holy Spirit, but the human spirit, an inner spiritual ability to be attuned to God. 1 Corinthians 14:14 tells us: *For if I pray in a tongue, my spirit prays but my mind is unfruitful*. Likewise 1Corinthians 2:11: says *For who knows a person's thoughts except the spirit of that person, which is in him?* 1Corinthians 5:3-5 elaborates on Paul's relation, through his spirit, to the Corinthian Church members: *For though absent in body, I am present in spirit; and as if present, I have already pronounced judgment on the one who did such a thing. When you are assembled in the name of the Lord Jesus and my spirit is present, with the power of the Lord Jesus, you are to deliver this man to Satan for the destruction of the flesh, so that his spirit may be saved in the day of the Lord.* In Romans 8:16, Paul says that: *The Spirit Himself bears witness with our spirit that we are children of God.*

So, our soul, our inner life, emotions and consciousness, our very essence, can be revived by God's Word. It can make us wise, as opposed to smart, and can rejoice our heart in delight. Our soul is a deeper and completely supernatural place compared to our heart or brain, a place to which the Holy Spirit has access, but science has no access. Psalms 103:1-2 says: *Bless the Lord, O my soul, and all that is within me, bless his holy name! Bless the Lord, O my soul, and forget none of his benefits.* Psalms 139:14: *I praise you, for I am fearfully and wonderfully made. Wonderful are your works; my soul knows it very well.*

Our supernatural soul has the ability to understand what baffles our brain and our scientists. Unlike our brain and heart, our soul is eternal (Matthew 10: 28: *And do not fear those who kill the body but cannot kill the soul. Rather fear him who can destroy both soul and body in hell*).

During life, our physical brain is accompanied by our physical body, just as throughout eternity, our spiritual soul will be accompanied by our spiritual body. In 1Corinthians 15: 44, Paul tells us that *It is sown a natural body; it is raised a spiritual body. If there is a natural body, there is also a spiritual body.*

Our Spirit

I Thessalonians 5:23 says: *Now may the God of peace Himself sanctify you completely, and may your whole spirit and soul and body be kept blameless at the coming of our Lord Jesus Christ..* Hebrews 4:12 says: *For the* Word *of God is living and active, sharper than any two edged sword, piercing to the division of soul and of spirit, of joints and of marrow, and discerning the thoughts and intentions of the heart.* The Trichotomy view of Plato, that man is made up of the physical body, the soul and the spirit, is supported by these texts... The Dichotomy view of Augustine and the Duality view of Thomas Aquinas say that man is made up of two constituents or parts, the soul or spirit (the true man or essence), and the body (a temporary abode for the soul).

The Trichotomy view, which separates the spirit as a different constituent, will define the spirit as that which knows and is capable of awareness and communication with God.

Our Mind

Our mind, according to Webster's, is *the element or complex of elements in an individual that feels, perceives, thinks, wills and especially reasons.* In this definition, *element* means a constituent part. Biblically, our mind is the faculty connected with intellectual understanding, as opposed to our spirit or soul which is discussed above.

Science has not been able to completely understand our mind, since like the soul, it is not natural or physical and cannot be dissected. Psychology attempts to understand the results of the functioning of our mind and psychoanalysts attempt to manipulate our mind to improve its functioning or make it more normal.

Even more so than for our brains, science has been unable to accurately determine whether our heredity, our environment, our God, or a combination, controls our mind. Our mind doesn't seem to be as deep as our soul since the mind functions as only an organizer of our experiences, in order to form thoughts that can result in actions or words.

The soul, on the other hand, can be removed by God (Luke 12: 19-20: *And I will say to my soul, 'Soul, you have ample goods laid up for many years; relax, eat, drink and be merry'. But God said to him, 'Fool! This night your soul is required of you, and the things you have prepared, whose will they be?'*.

Our God

Our God of course, can be far removed from our unregenerated minds, even though our minds seem to be supernatural. But we must assume that our minds will be a part of our resurrected bodies in Heaven; our souls and our spirits will certainly be.

God is the Creator of our complete being, spiritual and natural, and all that we are, with the exception of our sin nature, which Jesus has paid for with His blood, will live forever with the Trinity in Heaven.

What Does This Mean?

Many philosophers, writers and theologians have attempted to put some order into these basic categories of existence. There have been different conclusions, but most Christian thinkers seem to agree that Scripture does not appear to include a systematic distinction between physical and non-physical constituents; both are real and true. Ephesians 4:23 says: *and to be renewed in the spirit of your minds*. We sometimes want to distinguish between knowledge of head and of heart, but the Bible shows that we should believe, love and serve the Lord with all that is in us. The purpose in this book is to cause readers to consider the basic differences in natural and supernatural truth and be able to accept both. Otherwise, only a small part of truth will be recognized and our wisdom and interpretation of truth will be very limited.

The Existence of God

The existence of God is not denied by most laypeople and scientists but there is a large "militant atheism" movement at the present. A scientist is especially dishonest if he refuses to face the question of what created the *primal soup* or the original "intelligence". Whether the theory is of an ultra dense mass from which the *Big Bang* originated, or an intelligence, or meme that brought omnipresent matter together to form the first acetic acid or RNA, a never disproven law of science is that matter can be changed, but it cannot be created or destroyed. This law is being debated using theories such as the "mechanic theory" to justify how something can be formed from nothing, but the law remains valid.

Science and the governments of the world have spent billions of dollars in experimentation attempting to make living organisms from inorganics, and have failed. Even this futile attempt demonstrates the belief that a "designer" must control the formation of a complex structure. Scripture proves to us that this designer is God.

As Christians, it is not unusual to face a denial of logic and common sense related to the truth of the Bible. The Word says consistently that those claiming to be wise became fools and that their hearts were hardened so that they could not understand the truth. Romans 11: 8 says: *God gave them a spirit of stupor, eyes that would not see and ears that would not hear, down to this very day.* See also Deuteronomy 29:4, Psalms 94:11, Isaiah 6: 9-10, 29:10, 43:8, Jeremiah 5:21, Ezekiel 12:2, Matthew 13:14, John 12:40, Acts 28: 26-27, Romans 1:22, 11:8, 1 Corinthians 3:20, 2 Corinthians 4:13, Ephesians 4:18, Colossians 2:8, 2 Thessalonians 2:10-12, I Timothy 1: 6-7.

The Truth of the Bible

This book presupposes a belief in the inerrancy of Scripture. Deuteronomy 12:32: *Everything I command you, you shall be careful to do; you shall not add to or take from it;* Matthew. 5:18: *For truly, I say to you, until heaven and earth pass away, not an iota, nor a dot, will pass from the Law until all is accomplished";* Romans 15:4: *For whatever was written in former days was written for our instruction, that through endurance and through the encouragement of the Scriptures, we might have hope;* 2 Peter. 1:20,21: *Knowing this first of all, that no prophesy of Scripture comes from someone's own interpretation. For no prophesy was ever produced by the will of man, but men spoke from God as they were carried along by the Holy Spirit;* 2 Peter. 3:15-16: *Just as our beloved brother Paul also wrote to you, according to the wisdom given him, as he does in all his letters as he speaks in them of these matters. There are some things in them that are hard to understand, which the ignorant and unstable twist to their own destruction, as they do the other scriptures.* Indeed Paul tells us in 2 Corinthians 4:2: *But we have renounced disgraceful, underhanded ways. We refuse to practice cunning or to tamper with God's Word.* Revelation 22: 18-19: *I warn everyone who hears the prophesy of this book: if anyone adds to them, God will add to him the plagues described in this book.*

These verses speak to the inerrancy and infallibility of the Scriptures as inspired by God. For those readers who have difficulty believing that every word of the Bible is completely true, even though these verses support that belief (especially Matthew. 5:18 concerning the Old Testament and 2 Peter

3:16 concerning the New Testament), the following comments are offered:

- Virtually all organizations have a charter, a mission statement, by-laws or some sort of written documentation to describe their purpose. An organization which ignores or changes these standards becomes a different organization from the original. It is certainly reasonable, and in some cases best, to change founding documents when those documents provide the mechanism for amendment. A government can acquire a different purpose or better provide for its constituents; a company can improve or expand its service, products or profits; a religion can adapt to the times and attract more followers; but a Christian Church, if it ignores or changes the Bible, even in the slightest way, is on a slippery slope which, if left unchecked, will ultimately cause the church to lose its identity as a Christian Church. It has lost its complete founding document which was not written by founders but was written by the supernatural Founder. His document His Bible, allows no provision for amendment as explained above. Therefore a Christian Church which allows interpretation of the Holy Scriptures by man, instead of the Holy Spirit, has become a non-Christian sect, with man as its head, in place of God.
- The Bible must be understood in context, i.e. the Bible interprets the Bible. All of the popular

so called discrepancies in the Bible are taken out of context. For instance, there are books of history such as the Pentateuch (Genesis, Exodus, Leviticus, Numbers, Deuteronomy), then Joshua through Job; books of poetry and wise sayings such as Psalms, Proverbs, Ecclesiastes, and Song of Solomon; and books of prophesy, such as Isaiah through Malachi.
- In the new Testament, there are books of history, such as the gospels (Matthew, Mark, Luke and John), then The Acts of the Apostles; and letters such as Romans through Jude; and the prophetic book of Revelation.
- Most supposed contradictions come from either Proverbs or the Gospels. Proverbs, in context, is a book of wise and true sayings by Solomon, which, as in life today, teach one action or response in one case, and perhaps an opposite action or response in another case. The Gospels are written by observers who witnessed, or researched (Luke) and emphasized different and similar events.
- By virtually all definitions, God is supernatural, supreme, the creator, omniscient (has infinite knowledge), omnipresent (present everywhere at all times), omnipotent (has unlimited power), and omnibenevalent (has perfect goodness).
- A perfect God logically must do everything perfectly, or He wouldn't be God. This includes communication with His creation. He has elected to do that in the written form,

the most advanced technology of communication available at the time of the writings. The Hebrew people were appointed by God to copy the manuscripts as originally authored, Romans3:1-2: *Then what advantage has the Jew? Or what is the value of circumcision? Much in every way. To begin with, the Jews were entrusted with the oracles of God.* By law these scribes transcribed these manuscripts perfectly, or the manuscripts were destroyed. The success of this practice has been confirmed by comparing transcribed manuscripts discovered many centuries ago with those which were transcribed even earlier but not discovered until 1947 (the Dead Sea Scrolls).

- Christians, and Jews accepting Jesus Christ as their Savior, as the new Israel, are now responsible for preserving God's Holy Word. 1 Corinthians 4:1: *This is how one should regard us, as servants of Christ and stewards of the mysteries of God.* Romans 3:29-30: *Or is God the God of Jews only? Is He not the God of Gentiles also? Yes of Gentiles also, since God is one. He will justify the circumcised by faith and the uncircumcised through faith*; Romans 9:6-8: "*But it is not as though the Word of God has failed. For not all who are descended from Israel belong to Israel, and not all are children of Abraham because they are his offspring, but 'Through Isaac shall your offspring be named'. This means that it is not the children of the flesh who are the children of God, but the children of promise are counted as offspring.* (See also Hosea 2:23, Romans 9:24, 10:12; 11:25-27; 15:8-21, Galatians 4:28)

Therefore it is logical that a perfect and good God would communicate the truth of His desire to spend eternity with His creation in a perfect way, without error, and through His omnipotence, assure that translations are faithful as He intended.

Bible Translations

It is recommended that a study of the purpose of a translation be done before a literal interpretation of the words is made. For instance, some translations are intended to be literal, some are intended to be updated in language, some are paraphrases, and some are commentaries.

A Hebrew-English and Greek- English interlinear translation and a Hebrew and Greek/ English lexicon are helpful in understanding the translations, since the English language has fewer words for many of the words in the original languages of the Bible. i.e. three Hebrew words are translated as *love* in the much weaker English language. God selected Hebrew, Aramaic and Greek for a purpose.

Most quotes in this book are from the English Standard Version translation. This translation, as well as the King James, the New King James, the New American Standard and others are intended to be as literal as the English language allows.

The Rest of the Book

This book will delve into the issues expressed in this Chapter, hopefully providing readers with a background, or at least some thoughts, to proceed with a true view of what a Christian environmentalist could look like and act like.

Chapter 4
The Environment Today

*E*ach day we arise and follow pre-planned, or spontaneous activities, actions and reactions. We go to work, shop, exercise, meet with people, read, study, travel and perform many different functions for survival or pleasure. Nature affects and changes these normal activities with rain, heat, cold, catastrophic weather, etc.

Conversely, the human effects on nature can also affect our daily lives, when we become sick from environmental pollution, herbicides or pesticides, cannot afford fresh vegetables because of our urban location, cannot enjoy nature because of human desecration, or experience the effects of acid rain, smog or tobacco smoke.

Have you ever felt at one with nature? You can't be at one with nature, only with God. Nature, in its fallen state, can hurt or kill, when you least expect it.

But you can protect yourself from nature and at the same time, protect nature.

Since each of us is affected by the environment and also affects the environment, as Christians, we must make conscious decisions in our relationship to and with nature.

Biblically, we have been given dominion over the environment, just as we have dominion over our children. *Dominion*, according to Webster, is to rule, or have the power to rule. To *rule* means to have an influence over and to guide. So our dominion over nature, as over our children includes guidance. In this chapter we will examine the current state of the environment and the regulatory interests and trends.

As our surroundings, the environment consists of air, water, land, and the life or growth within these three realms.

Historically, the first governmental regulations to protect our surroundings were in reaction to air pollution events in England in the 14th century and the United States in 1948. This genesis of environmental concern is understandable since, of the three possible receptors for the by-products of civilization, air is the most sensitive and the most dispersing.

These residuals of human activity, whether in vapor, liquid or solid form, can be discharged into the air, water or the land, resulting in pollution, or they can be recycled for re-use. These pollutants, once discharged into one of these three receptors, are stored and remain in the receptor, are dispersed by the receptor and distributed over a wide area into another receptor, or are broken down chemically or biologically and converted into less harmful states, disposal or distribution.

Pollution of the Environment

The three realms of our natural environment receive un-natural organic and inorganic pollutants from the other realms as well as from the life or growth within the realms. These pollutants are transported from the realm in which they were created by natural processes or by human activities (which could be defined as natural activities just as well as animal activities), into a different realm or back into the same realm. These pollutants may be identical to their created form, or may be chemically altered by natural or human activities or processes. Some examples of such pollution are as follows:

Natural Pollutants

From Forests
- Carbon dioxide and hydrocarbons from rotting vegetation

From wild animals
- Carbon dioxide from breathing and death
- Methane from flatulence
- Hydrogen sulfide from flatulence
- Ammonia from urine
- Hydrocarbons and organics from death
- Inorganics and organics from erosion due to deforestation

From Volcanoes
- Carbon dioxide
- Hydrogen sulfide
- Methane
- Subterranean inorganics
- Inorganics and organics from erosion due to deforestation
- Pollution caused by temperature effects
- Pollution caused by flooding as a result of volcanic activity
- Pollution caused by animal deaths

From Earthquakes
- Pollution caused by death
- Pollution caused by deforestation

From Drought
- Pollution caused by death
- Pollution caused by deforestation

Human Caused Pollutants

From Breathing
- Carbon dioxide

From Cooking and Heating
- Hydrocarbons
- Carbon dioxide
- Particulates

The Environment Today

From Domestic Garbage and Trash
- Hydrocarbons
- Ammonia
- Hydrogen sulfide
- Carbon dioxide
- Inorganic metals
- Inorganic non-metals
- Paper Products
- Food wastes
- Chemical wastes
- Pharmaceuticals
- Endocrine disruptors

From Domestic Animals
- Carbon Dioxide from breathing and death
- Methane and hydrogen sulfide from flatulence
- Ammonia from urine
- Hydrocarbons and inorganics from death

From Agricultural Activities
- Pesticides
- Herbicides
- Nitrogen and phosphorous from fertilizer
- Hydrocarbons
- Erosion

From Industrial and Commercial Activities
- Hydrocarbons
- Carbon dioxide
- Inorganics; metals and non-metals
- Volatile organics
- Nuclear wastes

Air Pollution

From the beginning of civilization, cooking and heating have been the source of air pollution from the burning of animal, vegetable and petroleum based hydrocarbons, whether wood, peat, dung, fat, vegetable oil, animal oil, natural gas or coal. In the air, these hydrocarbons (organics), residual inorganic vapors, such as CO_2 and H_2S, and particulate pollutants receive no beneficial treatment, are not normally purified or broken down, but only dispersed, except for absorption and transfer to the ground by rainwater. Also inorganics such as NO, NO_2 and SO_2 can have thermal or photochemical reactions in the presence of oxygen and/or sunlight to form different compounds. There also can be reactions on the surface of particulates or in solution that cause some chemical changes.

In relatively recent years fluorinated hydrocarbons in the form of refrigerants, have become an air pollution concern.

Due to wind and thermal activity, this dispersion can be regional or international in scope. The dispersed pollutants can remain in the air permanently or at least for long periods of time, especially if they are vapors or gases. If the pollutants are lighter than air, or close enough to the specific gravity of air, they can rise or be carried higher in the atmosphere by wind and thermal currents. If the pollutants are particulates, or heavier than air, they can settle, or be carried by air movement, back to the surface. Therefore air pollution may be dispersed in the air, or carried to bodies of water, or the ground. The 1883 eruption of the Krakatoa volcano raised the average global temperature by as much as 2.2oF until 1888 (Wikipedia).

Nature itself contributes to air pollution through vegetative and animal decay and domestic and wild animals. It has been estimated that domestic animals use 30 percent of the world's ice free land, consume 8 percent of the world's fresh water and produce 18 percent of the world's greenhouse gases, which is more than all forms of transportation(1).

As a result of the environmental catastrophes experienced in the 1940's and 1950's, concern developed in the United States for the protection of public health. At that time, the responsibility for this concern was the Public Health Service, established in 1948.

Earlier environmental regulations in Europe and the United States were limited to control of burning coal in urban areas.

The Clean air Act in 1963 gave the U.S. Public Health Service, Department of Health, Education and Welfare (HEW), a role in handling air pollution and intervening in instances of health and welfare endangerment.

The Clean Air Act Amendments of 1965 let HEW set federal automotive emissions standards.

The Air Quality Act of 1967 allowed HEW to issue federal air quality criteria.

---

(1) "Meat from a Petri Dish", Scott Canon, Kansas City Star.

The Clean Air Act Amendments of 1970 resulted in the establishment of the Environmental Protection Agency (EPA). The EPA was required to set National Ambient Air Quality Standards primarily to protect health, and secondarily to protect welfare.

The most comprehensive air control legislation to date, was contained in the Clean Air Act Amendments of 1990 which addressed pollution from fixed and mobile sources, hazardous air pollutants, acid rain, operating permits and ozone protection. The Amendments listed six pollutants that were deemed critical in producing harmful effects to public health and welfare. These criteria pollutants were particulate matter, sulfur dioxide, ozone, nitrogen oxides, carbon monoxide and lead. These pollutants were nationally limited to certain concentrations, and the attainment of these standards continues to affect the local fixed and mobile source emission requirements in the entire country.

The rules restrict development which emits these priority pollutants unless the standards are met in the area. Regulatory authorities in the form of states or metropolitan areas, are required to enforce the priority pollutant emissions to assure that the National Ambient Air Quality Standards are met, or to lower the geographical area standards even below the established limits.

Acid rain, caused primarily by the oxides of sulfur and nitrogen from the combustion of fossil fuels, was also addressed by the 1990 Amendments

Mobile sources (automobiles, trucks, etc.), are included in these regulations. Other rules apply primarily to industries for control of hazardous air pollutants and apply to power plants to control acid rain. Rules also limit or prohibit certain ozone layer depleting chemicals.

Air pollution control rules continue to be issued, and presumably will continue to be issued in the future. New rules apply to specific industries, limiting certain appropriate pollutants to national standards. These standards are based on the Maximum Achievable Control Technology (MACT) experienced in these industries for the control of these pollutants. These regulations are expected to be continually issued in the future as more pollutants of concern are discovered by the EPA, and through risk analysis, health and environmental effects are better understood.

Green House Gases

Under the Ozone Protection title of the 1990 Clean Air Act Amendments, certain ozone depleting chemicals such as Freon have been regulated and/or eliminated to prevent destruction of the ozone layer which protects us from solar ultra violet radiation and the potential of global warming through the greenhouse effect.

Since the last few years of the twentieth century, even more concern has developed over the effect of green house gas (ghg) emissions on global warming and global climate change. In the 1970's the concern was for global cooling, in the 1980's and 1990's, that concern changed to global warming, and in the 2000's, the interest has been on climate change.

The greenhouse gas effect theorizes that the ozone layer in the stratosphere (up to 5 to 10 miles) collects ghg's which allow solar radiation to pass through, but restricts its return to the mesosphere (over 30 miles high), thereby increasing global temperatures, as in a greenhouse.

In 2009, when global temperatures plummeted, the concern changed again from global warming or cooling, to climate change, in order to explain the effect of weather, but not necessarily the cause of weather.

One theory is that regional warming, especially of certain areas of the ocean, can effect global climate, even if warming is not consistent. Much effort has been expended in relating cause and effect, and to date, the most reliable relationships have been either ghg's or solar activity. Global temperature has been graphed with man made carbon dioxide emissions, and carbon dioxide in the atmosphere. Both theories have had difficulty explaining radical variations in relationships from year to year, even though long term emission trends are reasonably consistent. Carbon dioxide (CO_2) has been selected for further study, since it is considered the most likely manmade ghg candidate.

A second concern for manmade CO_2 emissions arises from the realization that CO_2 can be sequestered (absorbed or stored) in only three ways; vegetation, bodies of water and soil. All non-sequestered CO_2 remains in the air.

All vegetation uses the Sun's photosynthesis as an electron donor and CO_2 as an electron acceptor to produce energy and emit oxygen. All animal life uses food as an electron donor and oxygen as an electron acceptor to produce energy source and emit CO_2. Therefore, the more vegetation that exists in an area, the more CO_2 sequestering and the less CO_2 accumulation in the air, water or land. Algae, an exception, act as a plant during the day, producing oxygen, and an animal at night, producing CO_2.

The land is a relatively insignificant sequestering agent for CO_2 since the bacteria in soil actually produce CO_2, and most soil CO_2 adsorption is actually absorption in the soil moisture.

The tendency for air to accumulate CO_2, as in most vapor/vapor mixing relationships, diminishes exponentially as the concentration in the air increases. This tendency drives more CO_2 to water surfaces. CO_2 in water forms carbonic acid, a weak acid which lowers the pH (the relative acidity) of the body of water. Lower water pH has been shown to negatively affect organic aquatic life including coral reefs. It should be emphasized though, that CO_2 is not the only killer of coral reefs. Warm water bleaching, and to an even greater extent, cold water bleaching, have also been shown to severely damage 200-300 year old coral in a span of 5 days (1).

This is an example of why we shouldn't emotionally attack certain possible causes of environmental

---

(1) *Coral Reefs*", Feb., 2012, the Journal of the International Society for Reef Studies, J.A. Kidney, J.M. Morrison, and V.B. Brinkhuis

damage without researching available scientific resources.

The absorption of CO2 into water vapor or droplets in the air, also lowers the pH of rain and dew and makes them more acidic. This tendency is accelerated if sulfur dioxide (SO2), is emitted into the air, forming sulfuric acid (H2SO4); if oxides of nitrogen (NOx) are emitted, forming nitric acid (HNO3); or if chlorine is emitted, forming hydrochloric acid (HCl). These strong acids, as well as CO2 are emitted by coal fired power plants, and other industrial sources, causing acid rain. The author has completed extensive research documenting rainfall and dew at pH levels as low as 3, downwind by around 100 miles from major coal fired power plants.

Global Warming

In the past decades, much effort has gone into global temperature predictions. The U.S. National Oceanic and Atmospheric Administration reports global land and ocean temperatures from about 1880 to the present. These records are accepted by virtually all climate scientists and show a recovery from the Little Ice Age for the annual global temperature from 1880 to 1930, from about 59oF to 61oF, a warm period of 61-62oF between 1930 and 1950, a cooling from 61-59oF between 1950 and 1970, and an up and down variable, but gradual warming from 1970 to the present, from 59 to 61oF. All temperatures are annual averages.

Temperature extremes and temperatures in different geographical areas, and ocean/land temperatures have varied much more during these periods. The difficulty in understanding global warming is not what has happened, but why. Scientists have related temperatures to atmospheric carbon dioxide, and to solar activity. CO2 has had an exponential rise, as expected, since the industrial revolution, as more fossil fuel is used for energy. CO2 has risen in a fairly smooth curve, but temperatures have been erratic with several periods of temperature drops while CO2 is increasing.

A much closer correlation has been found when comparing global temperatures with solar activity. From 1860 to the present there is a close fit as shown in *Environmental Effects of Increased Atmospheric Carbon Dioxide*, Journal of American Physicians and Surgeons (2007) 12, 79-90.

It appears that we are currently in a period of relatively mild global warming which is related more closely to solar activity than any other variable, but the continued increase in human caused CO2 emissions must be considered as a factor that will tend to increase, and certainly not decrease, global warning.

High solar activity is a combination of more solar flares, a strong solar wind, and more sunspots. The sun's electromagnetic field under active conditions, envelops the earth and shields it from galactic cosmic radiation, producing fewer clouds and a warmer earth (1).

---

(1) *Experimental Evidence for the Role of Ions in Particle Nucleation Under Atmospheric Conditions"*, *Proceedings from the Royal Society*, A.463 (2078): 385-396.

As explained further in Chapter 4, a more critical concern may be the gradual lowering of pH in oceans caused by CO_2 absorption.

Climate Change

Since global warming has been shown to be cyclical and more dependent on solar activity, recent concern has been centered around climate change. A summary of climate related events costing more than one billion dollars from 1980-2012 is as follows (NOAA):

- Of the 58 events from 1980-2003, 28% were hurricanes, 21% were non-tropical floods, 17% were heat waves or droughts and the rest were all under 10%, based on 2003 dollars.
- Of the 63 listed events since 2003, 22% were hurricanes, 11% were heat waves or droughts, and 44% were tornados, based on 2012 dollars.

Another interesting statistic from NOAA is the following Category 5 hurricanes by decade:

Decade	Number of Hurricanes, Cat. 5
1920's	1
1930's	3
1940's	1
1950's	4
1960's	6
1970's	3
1980's	3

1990's 2
2000's 8

Many of the more damaging hurricanes such as Sandy, Irene, Ike and Katrina were lower categories and the damage occurred mainly because of flood surge, length or population density. It is virtually impossible to objectively relate these natural disasters to human caused environmental conditions, since there is no consistency between the events and the amount of greenhouse gases, CO_2 or other pollution discharge.

It is probable that the earnest desire to relate human activity to environmental disasters is rooted in the need for many scientists to believe that we as a human race can affect and correct climate. The Bible teaches, and science confirms, that a supernatural intelligent source created the climate and the weather and we can protect ourselves from it, but cannot change it as seen below in Chapters 7 and 8.

Water Pollution

Mankind has normally disposed of liquid wastes in the water or on the ground. The most common receptor has always been the water, since its usual movement is away from the source of pollution.

The liquid, or even solid pollutants have historically resulted from eating, cooking, washing, feces and urine. Where moving streams and rivers are found, civilization develops, and solid wastes such as trash, garbage and feces have been dumped into these bodies of water for disposal. In the water, the hydrocarbon portion of these pollutants can be broken down by oxygen present in the water into carbon dioxide and water, but much of the time, the bacteria and the oxygen in the water are insufficient to completely break down these hydrocarbons.

Due to the oxidation, along with water movement, tides, or waves, water pollution, even though somewhat diminished through natural treatment, is normally only local or regional in scope. But still, organic pollutants can be distributed by the water.

Inorganic pollutants can remain in the water as widely distributed salts or dissolved chemicals, or float or settle in quiescent areas and collect as sediment in the bottom of streams, rivers or the ocean. Volatile organics, which can evaporate at certain temperatures, and certain volatile inorganics such as carbon monoxide and carbon dioxide, which are disposed of in bodies of water can return to the air.

During the same period that concern was developed over air pollution, water pollution was determined to be a health issue due to the realization that many communicable diseases such as cholera, typhoid, salmonellosis, amoebic dysentery, are water borne.

As in the case of air, water pollution concerns in the United States started with control by the Public Health Service and progressed to the EPA in 1970, when the environment was added as a regulatory issue.

As a result of the Clean Water Act of 1972, the EPA required regulatory agencies, which in most cases were states, to classify all navigable steams for their uses as navigation, recreation, irrigation, water supply and/or fish and wildlife. The EPA compiled results of a literature review of studies of water quality requirements for each of these stream uses.

Navigation pollutants included solids that were floatable or could otherwise interfere with navigation.

Protection of waters for *recreational* uses included pollutants which could be ingested through the skin or orifices.

Irrigation water use was protected by restricting the amount of sodium and other pollutants that can negatively affect plant life.

Water supplies were protected by limiting organic pollutants which were known or suspected to have negative health effects.

Fish and Wildlife is the category of environmental protection for aquatic life in receiving streams. Recommended permit levels were based on a literature review of toxicity test results on standard biological species such as fathead minnows and *sera daphnia*, a water flea. Other permit levels are based on toxicity to the environment from organic and inorganic pollutants with discharges expressed in concentration. The Act was written so that dilution of the concentration with clean water is not allowed (dilution is not the solution for pollution). A mass or weight per day limit has been established in most permits for this purpose. Underground water has been classified as surface water for the purpose of permitting.

The first emphasis on discharges was to issue permits for direct discharges to a stream., whether from municipal, industrial or private sources. These discharges typically enter a stream through one or more pipes or ditches. These sources were thought to include about 25 percent of the total water pollutants being discharged to U.S. streams.

Later, indirect discharges, such as contaminated stormwater carried in storm sewers, or running in sheet flow over the ground, were permitted for municipal, industrial and private sources. These indirect sources were thought to include another 25 percent of total pollutants.

The remaining 50 percent of discharged pollutants were thought to come from agricultural and undeveloped areas. The only agricultural non-manufacturing discharges typically regulated to date are animal feed lots.

The unregulated agricultural stormwater discharges contain agricultural chemicals such as fertilizer (primarily nitrogen and phosphorous), herbicides and pesticides. Undeveloped areas, fields and forests discharge unregulated pollutants into streams and underground reservoirs as by-products of vegetative and animal decay, animal wastes and inorganic metals and non metals. This last category of discharged water pollutants means that unregulated pollutants can be as high as 100 percent of the total pollutant load.

Land Pollution

The third receptor of pollutants, the land, throughout history, has been the only receptor of non vapor/ particulate pollution in arid areas, and certainly, along with water, the primary receptor in all areas of civilization. Even today, the edges of growing urban areas are used for land fills and garbage dumps for the by-products of the inner development.

Excrement has always been disposed of in latrines, privies, outhouses or on the surface of the ground.

Of the three pollutant receptors, the soil provides the only significant biological means of pollutant treatment (water can provide some minor biological treatment), in the form of cellular oxidation, using bacteria which can convert organics primarily into carbon dioxide, water, hydrogen sulfide, nitrogen forms and methane. Because of the relatively non-porous nature of soil, the result of soil pollution is normally local in concern, although in Karst terrain, which is permeated with fissures and caves, pollutants can potentially be transported regionally, either underground or when they reach surface waters.

The disposal of solid wastes on the ground doesn't guarantee their treatment, especially if these solids are placed into cells, such as in a landfill where they are not associated directly with the soil. Inorganics placed in the soil will normally remain as placed, which constitutes storage rather than treatment. I have excavated a 50 year old abandoned landfill and found readable newspapers and whole pieces of vegetation.

As expressed above, land or soil and its vegetation is a receptor of pollutant discharges from society. Vegetation, depending on its extent and its characteristics, can uptake liquids through transpiration primarily through its roots. The pollutants in these liquids are either filtered out or absorbed or transpirated into the stems, branches, trunks, leaves, blades, etc. Some pollutants, such as nitrogen, phosphorous and trace metals, act as nutrients to the vegetation, carbon dioxide acts as an electron acceptor, but some pollutants are toxic to the plants or accumulate within them, making the plants toxic to animals and humans.

Pollutants which are not absorbed by vegetation may be adsorbed onto particles of soil, either from the air or from stormwater or direct discharged flow. As explained above, bacteria in the soil can act to break down organic pollutants, ultimately into carbon dioxide and water. Bacteria have no effect on inorganic pollutants, other than valence change, or as anaerobic reducing agents affecting H2S, NH4, PO4,etc. These inorganic pollutants can be considered to "have returned to the soil", although not necessarily in locations and concentrations at which they were initially removed from the soil.

Another principal source of land contamination is leachate from landfills. When rainwater percolates through a landfill, it can dissolve pollutants and wash them out of the sides or bottom of the landfill. This is especially true with acid rain which more readily dissolves heavy metals. As mentioned above, sodium in water can blind the soil so that percolation, or the passage of water through soil, is inhibited. This can actually be an advantage in landfill leaching, but a huge disadvantage in agriculture.

Hydraulic Fracturing

Hydraulic fracturing is the practice of using water, sand and other additives pumped under high pressure into underground shale formations in order to create fractures in the shale in order to allow natural gas to be removed. In the United States, which consumes almost 25% of the world's oil products, the fracturing technology has the potential to supply the U.S. energy demand for between 90 and 116 years (1). This method of natural gas extraction has the capacity to make this country independent of foreign oil until non petroleum energy becomes feasible. The technology is rather old, beginning in shallow wells in the 1860's, advancing with acid etching in the 1930's, to hydraulic fracturing in 1947, and "slickwater" fracturing in 1997.

The method of horizontal drilling can make natural gas deposits from 5,000 to 20,000 feet deep available for economical removal Environmental concerns include air pollution in the form of methane emissions, migration of the fracturing fluid into underground water aquifers, and the release and/or disposal of spent fluids on the surface. The most

---

(1) *Modern Shale Gas Development in the United States, a Primer*, U.S. Department of Energy, April 2009).

widely used chemicals in fracturing are methanol, isopropyl alcohol, 2-butoxyethanol, ethylene glycol and proprietary chemicals such as resin sand coating, polymers, oxidizers, gels and salts. These are normal industrial chemicals and there is technically no reason they cannot be treated or reused without environmental contamination.

The methanol discharged into the air is no more of an air pollution concern than methanol from livestock flatulence and natural anaerobic organics decomposition.

Environmentally, this technology has advanced to the point that the risk from pollution seems to be less than many other industrial sources and well worth the effort to control with reasonable regulations, because of the huge energy benefit involved.

Regulatory Trends

The EPA has vacillated between a risk based and a mass or concentration based approach to regulations, and in the last few years has generally settled on mass based for air pollutants, concentration based for the health effects from water pollution, risk based for the environmental effects from water pollution, and concentration based for soil pollution.

Before the 1960's, health based regulations were developed epidemiologically from known sicknesses and deaths. When the interest, especially in water, was changed to the environment, risk based studies using lethal tests on minnows and water fleas were developed and have become the basis for most environmental regulations to minimize water pollution.

As explained previously, in 1990 the first regulated air pollutants were the six priority pollutants which were mass based limited because of observed health effects. Gradual regulatory additions have included health based regulations for mobile sources and environmental based mass limits for acid emitting industries. In the last few years, emphasis has been on industry specific technology based mass limits (MACT, Maximum Achievable Control Technology Standards). These regulations are the result of actual emissions from the most efficient industries within a category.

In air pollution control, there have been efforts to allow dischargers which lower emissions below regulatory levels, to sell or trade these credits on the open market. This effort has had mixed success but is still a potential for future approaches to environmental control.

Soil pollution has been regulated with the assumption that all pollutants discharged into the soil without being chemically fixed into the soil, will end up in groundwater. The discharge standards into water are therefore adopted for soil for toxic pollutants. Non-cumulative (in the body) inorganic pollutants are usually allowed to be put into the soil if they are naturally present at higher levels.

In the effort to force soil restoration, the EPA has classified much industrial property as SWMU's (Solid Waste Management Units), which usually require corrective action in the form of clean-up to background levels, before the property use is changed from industrial, and to prevent the pollutants from migrating offsite. Unfortunately, the enforcement of these regulations has been more on "mom and pop" gas stations than large industries with more serious pollution.

Before property is sold, more sophisticated buyers will require an Environmental Site Assessment (ESA) by a Professional Engineer to determine the level of pollution and environmental risks of the property. This is not typically a federal regulation, but a "due diligence" step by the buyers or financial lenders.

Even this effort has been abused. I was hired by a bank to do an ESA on a property going into foreclosure which had a previous ESA. I was surprised to see an obvious old city landfill on about 10% of the property, which had been ignored in the previous ESA. Such experience indicates that we should select environmental professionals carefully and not require of them certain conclusions.

There has been recent political rhetoric about eliminating the EPA because of its impact on job retention and creation. In my opinion, this would be a major mistake. The EPA does need to be reorganized and it should become a purely technical agency of the government instead of a political tool. It should be forced to coordinate and communicate more closely with state environmental departments which are closer to the issues.

In 1999 I was asked by state regulatory officials to volunteer my services to the successful presidential candidate as Director of the EPA Several U.S.

The Environment Today

Senators and Representatives were helping in these efforts. As part of the process, I did an extensive study of the organization of the EPA and wrote a paper which included detailed recommendations for improvements. I recommended that EPA should be managed by environmental professionals rather than politicians. The result of the following election was that a state governor was appointed to the position, rather than a professional.

It appears, based on environmental progress during the subsequent years, that EPA has been used as a political tool by the federal government administration as much as it has been a tool for cleaning up the environment. It would be a pleasure to see the EPA, OSHA, the IRS, the FCC, the FAA and the DOT rise above the political stranglehold and become purely professional services to our country.

The regulatory process of the U.S Government is for the Congress to pass laws requiring the appropriate agency to propose and promulgate rules and regulations through which the law is implemented. The law usually has a time deadline for the rules and regulations to be published, and many times this deadline is too soon for the agency to complete its research and adopt standards.

The EPA, in its attempt to be professional, many times will take more time than is allowed by the law to publish these rules and regulations. In these cases, environmental groups will typically sue the EPA to force them to proceed immediately to publish the regulations required by law, apparently believing that a poor law is better than no law at all. These lawsuits are usually successful since the EPA has not complied with the time requirements of the law. The EPA is then forced to speed up its process and many times has, in its haste, published regulations which are inadequately researched and developed and may be unenforceable. The result is usually a net slowdown of environmental protection caused by the unnecessary lawsuits. In my opinion, the environmental progress of our country would be years ahead if the EPA were allowed to complete its regulatory development work without interference.

An example of how outside influences affect the progress of environmental restorative efforts, is a comment I heard from an EPA employee who indicated that the issue which has slowed their regulatory progress more than any other, was the publication of books and numerous speeches by a former elected high official of the federal government, which over emotionalized the global warming issue, rather than allowing science to dictate regulatory decisions.

Chapter 5
God Speaks Out About the Environment

I grew up being educated to believe that God created our universe and has left it alone since that time. That safe belief allowed me to live my life thinking that I can enjoy God's beautiful Creation in its evolved state and to fall into the comfortable socio-academic mainstream belief system.

My wife Marion and I were teaching a 7th grade Sunday School class the different views of evolution and creation. I privately considered myself a theistic evolutionist because of my background in science and my educational indoctrination.

One of the students asked me to explain what I thought about this controversy. Fortunately the class was about over and I told him I would let the class know the following week.

I asked my pastor if he had any literature on the subject and he inundated me with books and articles. I believe that God spoke to me through my student and pastor and that literature, because this comfortable Christian changed that week from a theistic evolutionist to a creationist.

I thank God that my recent Master of Science in Environmental Engineering enabled me at that time to understand the futility of evolutionism, the proofs for creationism, and my membership in a strong Bible believing church gave me the resources to understand these theological resources, especially as they are expressed in the Bible.

Since that week when I told the 7th graders that I had changed my belief system, I have read and collected hundreds of books and articles on evolution and creation and taught the subjects several times. The reason that this experience is important in this book on the environment, is that God created the environment, and in His description of that Creation, He gave us directions concerning our responsibility. The following is a summary of what I believe God showed me during that week and in the 30 or so years since:

- I now firmly believe from a theological and a scientific basis that God created our universe in six literal days in the order expressed in Genesis 1 from things not visible, and that it was good. Hebrews 11:3 says: *By faith we understand that the universe was created by the word of God, so that what is seen was not made out of things that are visible.*

- I believe that before the sun was created on the fourth day as our measure of time, these literal days may have been of any length, but that God could just as well have made each of the six days of equal length in accordance with sun time.
- I believe that God created everything with apparent age so that it could function initially as designed and not have to grow into that ability.
- I believe that God inspired the Bible with words that communicate equally to any believer regardless of education or experience, through the Holy Spirit.

As explained in the previous chapters, God has chosen to communicate with us through his inspired written word which most Christians believe is the inerrant and infallible record of that communication. If this were not true in totality, we would be free to pick and choose which parts of the Bible are true and which are false. Then everyone would have his own Bible which would speak exclusively to him and we would discount the verses mentioned in the section titled *The Truth of the Bible* in Chapter 1, which are the basis for our belief. The purpose of this chapter is to examine some of the verses of the Bible in which God discusses the environment and our relation to it.

Organics and Inorganics

In the previous chapters of this book, the idea of the world being created as inorganics and organics is presented. In Undergraduate School, I barely existed through my Chemistry courses, which, along with High School Chemistry, taught me more about memorization skills than science. I am deeply indebted to Dr. George W. Malaney, who in Graduate School finally explained Chemistry in a way that was not only understandable, but fascinating. He started with the basics, and "taught" us, as opposed to "training" us.

So, this chapter is a basic summary of some of the principals of inorganic and organic chemistry to introduce the science that God created and described in His Word. The Bible, when studied as a whole, makes it clear that God originally created inorganics in the form of metals and non metals, and then created non-living and living organics in the form of inert compounds, vegetables and animals. This chapter will follow God's description of the inorganic and organic matter that was created, the way this creation was intended to be used and preserved by mankind, and the exciting preservation of His pre-Fall Creation in Heaven.

In general, inorganics are ions, elements, molecules and compounds of elements which do not contain both hydrogen and carbon (hydrocarbons). Hydrogen is a constituent of all acids and bases and of water. A few carbon containing compounds and ions such as cyanide (CN), carbon monoxide (CO), carbon dioxide (CO_2), carbonate (CO_3), and carbonic acid (H_2CO_3) are considered inorganic carbon compounds (the acid because it completely breaks down in water).

Some have defined organics as compounds of a biological origin or containing organic life, but that definition eliminates the most basic organic hydrocarbons of methane, and its derivatives which contain more carbon and/or hydrogen ions. They can originate from organics but are not biological life.

A sub category of organics must therefore be living and non-living, where living organisms are biological organisms containing DNA, RNA and proteins, which are subject to stimuli, and will reproduce, grow, develop and sustain themselves. A further sub category of living organics must be plants and animals. Animals can typically move spontaneously and independently and ingest other organisms for sustenance.

There is a commonality in all matter in that matter consists entirely of molecules. Living organic matter has a further commonality in that it contains very complex molecules of DNA and RNA which literally program the living organisms to be plants or animals, to be of a certain species, to have certain inherited characteristics, and to adapt to environmental changes.

This quick background in chemistry and biochemistry should form a basis for the truth revealed in the Bible, which Christians have been provided by God through His inspired human writers, interpreters and transcribers.

The following is a summary of God's description of each of the six days of Creation as the environment comes into being by His word.

Day One of Creation
The Earth

The first mention of the environment in the Bible is in Genesis 1:1: *In the beginning, God created the heavens and the earth.* This verse tells us that the environment is a creation of God from the beginning of time.

Romans 1:20 says: *For His invisible attributes, namely* His *eternal power and divine nature, have been clearly perceived, ever since the creation of the world, in the things that have been made. So they are without excuse.*

Genesis 1:2 tells us that the earth at that time: *was without form and void, and darkness was over the face of the deep. And the Spirit of God was hovering over the face of the waters.* 2 Peter 3:5 says that: *the earth was formed out of water and through water by the* Word *of God.* Job 26:7 says that God: *stretches out the north over the void and hangs the earth on nothing.*

Psalms 104:5-6 says that God: *set the earth on its foundations, so that it should never be moved"* and that He: *covered it with the deep.* See also Amos 5:8.

Therefore on Day 1, God created inorganics in the form of a mineral core covered with water.

On the first day, God also created light and darkness which He called day and night. *(Genesis 1:3-5: And God said 'Let there be light', and there was light. And God saw that the light was good. And God separated the light from the darkness. God called the light Day, and the darkness He called Night).* The sun was not created until the fourth day (verses 14-18: *And God said 'Let there be lights in the expanse of the heavens to separate the day from the night. . .And God made the two great lights-the greater light to rule the day and the lesser light to rule the night- and the stars. And God set them in the expanse of the heavens to give light on the earth).* Apparently, the light of the first day was the same light which Revelation describes in chapter 21, verse 23 as light of the Lamb Jesus: *And the city has no need for sun or moon to shine on it, for the glory of God gives it light, and its lamp is the Lamb.* There was no need for the sun or the moon, for a superior spiritual light shone.

Since Jesus was present at Creation, (John 1:1: *In the beginning was the Word*), and Jesus is designated as the Word (John 1: 1-5: *and the Word was with God, and the Word was God. He was in the beginning with God. All things were made through Him, and without Him was not anything made that was made. In Him was life, and the life was the light of men. The light shines in the darkness, and the darkness has not overcome it.;* 1 John 1: 1-4: *That which was from the beginning, which we have heard, which we have seen with our eyes, which we looked upon and have touched with our hands, concerning the word of life- the life was made manifest, and we have seen it, and testify to it and proclaim to you the eternal life which was with the father and was made manifest to us- that which we have seen and heard we proclaim also to you, so that you too may have fellowship with us; and indeed our fellowship is with the Father and with His son Jesus Christ.*), we can be assured that His word as communicated to us through the Holy Scriptures in both testaments, is true and without error.

Day Two of Creation
The Sky

On Day Two, Genesis 1:6-8, God created the sky (*"heaven"* or "firmament") and caused it to separate the waters underneath (the global ocean) and the waters above (the atmospheric water): *And God said 'Let there be an expanse in the midst of the waters, and let it separate the waters from the waters'. And God made the expanse and separated the waters that were under the expanse from the waters that were above the expanse. And it was so. And God called the expanse Heaven.* Psalms 104:6-7 speaks of God's rebuke which caused the waters to flee and the mountains to rise, to set boundaries for the waters: *You covered it with the deep as with a garment; the waters stood above the mountains. At* Your *rebuke they fled; at the sound of* Your *thunder they took to flight.*

So far, God has spent two days creating inorganic matter in the form of water and minerals as the part of the environment which cannot chemically be created, destroyed or broken down into organics containing carbon and hydrogen. There was as yet, no rain (Genesis 2:5) or organics, and unlike the next four days, God did not pronounce these days "good".

Day Three of Creation
Vegetation

On the third day of creation, described in Genesis 1:9-13, God separated the dry land from the seas and created the first organics, vegetation in the form of plants of sufficient apparent age to yield seed, and fruit trees of sufficient apparent age to yield fruit with seeds: *And God said, 'Let the waters under the heavens be gathered together into one place, and let the dry land appear'. And it was so. God called the dry land Earth, and the waters that were gathered together,* He *called Seas. And God saw that it was good. And God said 'Let the earth sprout forth vegetation, plants yielding seed, and fruit trees bearing fruit in which is their seed, each according to its kind, on the earth'. And it was so. The earth brought forth vegetation, plants yielding seed according to their own kinds, and trees bearing fruit in which is their seed, each according to its kind. And God saw that it was good.*

These plants and fruit trees were created, not as seeds, but as renewable plants yielding seed and fruit. Did the trees have rings, indicating age, when they were created? Probably, since they were trees and not some pre-historic semblance of trees.

For the first time, God said that His Creation was good. Even though Genesis 2:5 says that there was no rain at this time, there was a mist from the earth which watered the whole earth (Genesis 2:5-6: *When no bush of the field was yet on the land and no small plant of the field had yet sprung up- for the Lord God had not caused it to rain on the land, and there was no man to work the ground, and a mist was going up from the land and was watering the whole face of the ground*).

There was also no sun, therefore no photosynthesis to allow the plants to grow. But God's perfect light and *the river of the water of life* will allow vegetation in Heaven (Revelation 22:2: *through the middle of the street of the city; also on either side of the river, the tree of life, with its twelve kinds of fruit, yielding its fruit each month*), just as it did in Genesis 1:2. Genesis 2:5 also addresses the importance of man in relation to the vegetation of the environment since there was no: *man to work the ground*.

God had a purpose and a plan for His vegetative creation. Deuteronomy 20:19-20 says: *Whenever you besiege a city for a long time, making war against it in order to take it, you shall not destroy its trees by wielding an axe against them. You may eat from them but you shall not cut them down. Are the trees in the field human, that they should be besieged by you? Only the trees that you know are not trees for food you may destroy and cut down, that you may build siegeworks against the city that makes war with you, until it falls.*

If the third day of Creation were billions of years long, as evolutionists teach, these plants would have quickly died with no physical sun to allow photosynthesis (Day 4), and no insect to pollinate (Day 6).

God not only spoke of His vegetative creation in Genesis, but He made man so interdependent on vegetation that the entire Bible is filled with references as to how we should co-exist with plants. This relationship is not limited to the Bible's communication with mankind in an agricultural society, but is today every bit as important as it was when it was initially written.

It is significant that when God gave David the plans for His Temple, the details included beams, planks and walls of cedar, cherubim and doors of olivewood, floors and doors of cypress, and had carved into the wood cherubim (celestial beings, probably angels which originally guarded the Garden of Eden, and now guarded the Ark of the covenant), gourds, palm trees and open flowers. 1 Chronicles 28:19: *All this He made clear to me in writing from the hand of the Lord, all the work to be done according to the plan* (David's charge to Solomon).

So God demonstrated the relationship of His created cherubim, plants, trees and flowers to His chosen people by memorializing their figures in His Temple, even in the Inner Sanctuary (the Holy of Holies). These figures were not those of a god to be worshipped like Aaron (Exodus 32:4), Solomon (1Kings 11:7-8), and Jeroboam (1Kings 12:28) did.

Therefore God has made it clear that there is no Mother Nature or Mother Earth to worship; there is no other God before Him. All of our worship must be reserved for the Lord, but we can certainly learn of His creation and therefore His mercy and character by studying nature and working to preserve it for future generations.

Day Four of Creation
The Universe and Time

On the fourth day of Creation, described in Genesis 1: 14-19 as quoted above, God provided for time, as defined by the rotation of the earth and the movement of the sun and stars. Genesis 1:14 says that the purpose of the: *lights in the expanse of the heavens* was *to separate the day from the night,* and to be: *for signs, and for seasons, and for days and years,* and for light, all for the benefit of His animal and vegetation creation.

Psalms 104: 19-20 says that God: *made the moon to mark the seasons; the sun knows its time for setting. You made darkness and it is night.* He says in Genesis 1:18 that this part of His Creation was good, presumably since these lights function to serve the organic environment of the earth.

This stated purpose of the creation of the heavens speaks to the futility of man's obsession with discovering life outside of the earth. Jeremiah 10:2 says: *Learn not the way of the nations, nor be dismayed at the signs of the heavens because the nations are dismayed at them.*

Jeremiah 31:35-37 says: *Thus says the Lord, Who gives the sun for light by day, and the fixed order of the moon and the stars for light by night,... If this fixed order departs from before Me, declares the Lord, then shall the offspring of Israel cease from being a nation before me forever. Thus says the Lord; if the heavens above can be measured, and the foundations of the earth below can be explored, then I will cast off all the offspring of Israel for all that they have done.*

Jeremiah 33: 25-26 says: *Thus says the Lord; 'If I have not established* My *covenant with day and night and the fixed order of heaven and earth, then I will reject the offspring of Jacob and David My servant.*

Psalms 148: 1-6 says: *Praise the Lord! Praise the* Lord from the heavens; *praise* Him *in the heights!*

Praise Him *all* His *angels; praise* Him *all* His *hosts! Praise* Him *sun and moon, praise* Him *all you shining stars! Praise* Him *you highest heavens and you waters above the heavens! Let them praise the name of the Lord! For* He *commanded and they were created. And* He *established them forever and ever;* He *gave a decree, and it shall not pass away.*

Before this fourth day, there was nothing to differentiate between *days* and *years*; no sun to measure a 24 hour day or a 3 month season.

In the spiritual world, there is no sun or other means of measuring time. In fact, Psalms 90:4 says that to God: *a thousand years in your sight are but as yesterday when it is past, or as a watch in the night.*, and 2 Peter 3:8 says that: *with the Lord one day is as a thousand years, and a thousand years as one day.* Job 36:26 says: *Behold, God is great, and we know* Him *not; the number of* His *years in unsearchable.*

This lack of time in the spiritual world may also speak to predestination, prophesy (*Behold the former things have come to pass, and new things I now declare; before they spring forth I tell you of them.*, Isaiah 42: 9), and the timing of the return of Jesus, (1 Thessalonians 4: 15: *For this we declare to you by a word from the Lord, that we who are alive, who are left until the coming of the Lord, shall not precede those who have fallen asleep*).

The absence of spiritual time also calls to question the length of time of the first 3 days of Creation, since there was no way to measure time without a sun. Many Christian evolutionists argue that the Hebrew word translated *day*, in Genesis can mean an era, daylight, or a 24 hour day. Indeed, the Hebrew word *yom*, can be found translated in the Bible as *day* for all of these meanings.

But the weakness of this theological evolutionary argument is that the words *The evening and the morning* used for all six days of creation, are not used elsewhere in the Bible for any meaning other than the end and beginning of a 24 hour day (A study of Strong's Exhaustive Concordance shows that e*vening* is used for the end of a 24 hour day in all 52 times in the Old Testament that the word is used, and in all 7 times in the New Testament that the word is used. Likewise, *morning* is used in the Bible for the beginning of a 24 hour day all 207 times it is found in the Old Testament, and all 17 times it is found in the New Testament).

Besides Genesis 1 stating that Creation lasted six days with mornings and evenings, Exodus 20:11 again states: *For in six days the Lord made heaven and earth, the sea and all that is in them, and rested on the seventh day. Therefore the Lord blessed the Sabbath day and made it holy.* This passage, as well as the context expressed in verses 7-10 of Exodus 20, clearly describe six 24 hour days.

One theory of time during at least the first two days, is that in accordance with Einstein's Theory of Relativity, **E=MC2**, where E is energy, M is mass, and C is the speed of light, Creation, requiring infinite energy to produce mass from nothing, with an initially small mass (the earth), would cause the speed of light to be infinitely large.

An infinitely large or fast speed of light would explain the apparent age of the universe and the large number of light years it spans.

An infinitely large mass, after the fourth day of creation, along with an infinitely large energy, would make the speed of light apparently lowered to its current constant rate of 186,282 miles per second, since infinite energy keeps infinite mass moving without further creation.

At this relatively slow speed of light, we seem to see objects in the universe that existed millions or billions of years ago. But in the first two or three days of Creation, the infinitely fast speed of light would have allowed the sight of these far away objects to travel to the earth immediately.

Thus the breadth of the universe may indeed be billions of our current light years across, but the actual age of the universe may be only in the thousands of years, as the Bible insinuates. Only God can tell us whether Einstein's theory is true, and how it might vary through distant space and into the ancient past, but man has yet to disprove the theory. Also, only God can know whether these first days were very long or lasted only the 24 hours of our "sun days".

If we really believe in an omnipotent God, it must be accepted that He could have spoken the universe into existence in 6 days or 6 seconds. Revelation 4:11 says: *for* You *created all things, and by your will they existed, and were* (not 'are') *created*. This miracle of quick creation by God's word is no more supernatural than Jesus changing water into wine, raising

Lazarus from the dead, being born to a virgin, or being resurrected from the dead and ascended into Heaven.

Day Five of Creation
Aquatic Life and Birds

On the fifth day of Creation (Genesis 1: 20-23), God created living creatures for the first time in the water and the air: *And God said, 'Let the waters swarm with swarms of living creatures, and let birds fly above the earth across the expanse of the heavens.' So God created the great sea creatures and every living creature that moves, with which the waters swarm, according to their kinds, and every winged bird according to its kind*. He again stated that *it was good*.

It should be noted that before Day Five, Genesis 1 does not mention the word *living*, but beginning in verse 20, the start of the fifth day, *living* or *life*, is used to describe fish (verse 20,21), animals (verse 24), insects (verse 30), and man (Genesis 2:7). See also 1 Corinthians 15:45: *Thus it is written 'The first man, Adam, became a living being; the last Adam became a life- giving spirit.*

Science recognizes inorganics, non living organics, such as oil and gas, and living organics, such as plants and animals. But God seems to be describing *living* animals as a higher level of organics than plants. The theory of evolution has difficulty with the origin and interrelation of plant and animal life, but God is clear on the differentiation between these parts of Creation.

Day Six of Creation
Animals and Man

The sixth day brought about the creation of living creatures according to their kind on the earth including domestic animals (cattle), creeping things (presumably insects), and wild animals (beasts), and pronounced them good in Genesis 1: 24-25: *And God said 'Let the earth bring forth living creatures according to their kinds-livestock and creeping things and beasts of the earth according to their kinds'. And it was so. And God made the beasts of the earth according to their kinds and the livestock according to their kinds, and everything that creeps on the ground according to its kind. And God saw that it was good.* Note that God made livestock as separate creatures from the beasts of the earth, rather than domestic animals evolving from or being tamed from wild beasts. Psalms 104:30, says that when God sent forth His Spirit, they (all creatures) were created and God renewed the face of the earth. (see also Deuteronomy 4:32, Job 10: 8-11, Psalms 100:3, Ecclesiastes 11:5, Isaiah 45: 12, Jeremiah 27:5).

That same sixth day, in Genesis 1: 26 God states that He created: *man in* Our (plural) *image, after* Our *likeness*. Also Genesis 5:1: *when God created man*, He *made him in the likeness of God,* and Genesis 9:6b: *for God made man in* His *own image*. This is the first of Creation to bear God's image and likeness. Genesis 1: 27 says that He created man as *male and female* (see also Genesis 2:18, 5:2, Matthew 19:4).

In 1 Corinthians 11:8, Paul says: *For man was not made from women, but woman from man.* It is clear in this verse, as in many others, that Paul believed literally the words of Genesis, specifically Genesis 2:18-23: *Then the Lord God said 'it is not good that the man should be alone, I will make him a helper fit for him'. Now out of the ground the Lord God had formed every beast of the field and every bird of the heavens. . .But for Adam there was not found a helper fit for him. So the Lord God caused a deep sleep to fall upon the man, and while he slept took one of his ribs and closed up its place with flesh. And the rib that the Lord God had taken from the man, He made into a woman.* God created man and woman sequentially, just as He created all inorganics and organics sequentially by His Word.

Chapter 6

God's Purpose for Mankind

Dust and God's Breath

God made man out of dust (Genesis 2:7: *then the Lord God formed the man of dust from the ground and breathed into his nostrils the breath of life, and the man became a living creature*), and beasts and birds also out of the ground (Genesis 2:19: *So out of the ground the Lord God formed every beast of the field and every bird of the heavens*). He made woman out of man's rib (Genesis 2:22, 23: *And the rib that the Lord God had taken from the man He made into a woman and brought her to the man. Then the man said 'This at last is bone of my bones and flesh of my flesh; she shall be called Woman, because she was taken out of Man'*). (This could speak to the potential of stem cells.). In the same way, God gave breath from dust to animals, but with a different result: (Ecclesiastes 3:19-21: *For what happens to the children of man and what happens to the beasts is the same; as one dies, so dies the other. They all have the same breath and man has no advantage over the beasts, for all is vanity. All go to one place. All are from the dust, and to dust all return. Who knows whether the spirit of man goes upward and the spirit of the beast goes down into the earth?* Dust plus God's breath made man a living being (Genesis 2:7, 7:22, Job 33:4, Isaiah 42:5, Acts 17: 25). Inorganics plus God's breath equals living organics. When we die, we return to dust (Genesis 3:19: *By the sweat of your face you shall eat bread, till you return to the ground, for out of it you were taken; for you are dust, and to dust you shall return*), with God breaking down organics into inorganics and transferring our living soul from earth (our natural world) to Heaven and the new earth (our spiritual world) (Revelation 21:1).

Genesis 1: 28, still in the sixth day, says that God says they (male and female) should: *Be fruitful and multiply and fill the earth and subdue it and have dominion over the fish of the sea and over the birds of the heavens and over every living thing that moves on the earth*. Likewise Psalms 8:6-8 says that God gave man: *dominion over the works of your hands: you have put all things under* His *feet, all sheep and oxen, and also the beasts of the field, the birds of the heavens, and the fish of the sea.*

God tells Adam and Eve that He has given them every herb that yields seed which is on the face of the earth, and every tree whose fruit yields seed for food. He also to every beast of the earth and to every bird of the heavens and to everything that creeps on the earth, everything that has the breath of life: *has given every green plant for food* (Genesis 1:30). God therefore created plants as providers of food for man and animals, whose internal systems convert that food to energy, which eventually is recycled back to the plants in the form of carbon dioxide.

God also provided plants and animals to help us learn about His Creation and the wonder of nature. Solomon, the wisest man who has ever existed: *spoke of trees, from the cedar that is in Lebanon to the hyssop that grows out of the wall. He spoke also of beasts, and of birds, and of reptiles, and of fish. And people of all nations came to hear the wisdom of Solomon, and from all the kings of the earth, who had heard of his wisdom* (1 Kings 4:33-34, see also Job 38-41, Proverbs 30: 15-31, Matthew 6: 25-34).

Then in Genesis 1:31, God saw everything that he had made and called it *very good*. This is the first day that God used the adverb *very* to describe *good*. Thus God was satisfied with His creation of humans, and so should we be. Paul said: *I praise* You *for I am fearfully and wonderfully made* (Psalm 139:14). This wonderful creation is described as God's temple (I Corinthians 3:16-17: *Do you not know that you are God's temple and that God's Spirit dwells in you? If anyone destroys God's temple, God will destroy him. For God's temple is holy and you are that temple.* I Corinthians 6:19: *Or do you not know that your body is a temple of the Holy Spirit within you, whom you have from God? You are not your own, for you were bought with a price. So glorify God in your body.*)

Man and woman were a different creation than, not evolved from, the previously created animals. 1Corinthians 15:39 says: *For not all flesh is the same, but there is one kind for humans, another for animals, another for birds, and another for fish.*

The Bible tells us that the creation of man was not the result of evolution through various species, or even an afterthought of God to perfect His species, but was God's plan before the foundation of the world (Romans 8:29-30: *For those whom* He *foreknew,* He *also predestined to be conformed to the image of* His *Son, in order that* He *might be the firstborn among many brothers. And those whom* He *predestined* He *also called, and those whom* He *called* He *also justified, and those whom* He *justified* He *also glorified*".

Also 1 Peter 1:1-2: *Peter, an apostle of Jesus Christ, to those who are elect exiles. . .according to* the *foreknowledge of God the Father.* Romans 11:2: *God has not rejected* His *people whom* He *foreknew,* 2 Timothy 1:9: Who *saved us and called us to a holy calling, not because of our works but because of* His *own purpose and grace, which* He *gave us in Christ Jesus before the ages began).*

Man's Service to the Environment

The verses of the first chapter of the Bible describe God's gift of vegetation and fruit to mankind and animals for food (also Genesis 2:9: *And out of the ground the Lord God made to spring up every tree that is pleasant to the sight and good for food)*. This food producing vegetation was watered by a river (Genesis 2:10: *A river flowed out of Eden to water the garden*) because of the mist (Genesis 2:6). But this irrigation was insufficient to maintain the garden that God had planted, so he put man in the garden to *work it and keep it* (Genesis 2: 15).

From the third day to the sixth day man was not present to till the ground (Genesis 2:5). So, not only between Day 3 and Day 4 was there no sun, but between Day 3 and Day 6, there were no insects to pollinate, and no man to till the soil. Again, long day theories fail to explain this obviously very short period that vegetation could have possibly existed between Days 3 and 4.

This initial responsibility of man to till the ground was very crucial in the early days, prior to the universal flood because both man and animals were vegetarian. Genesis 2:16 says that God commanded Adam to freely *eat of every tree of the Garden* of Eden. In Genesis 3:18, as part of the curse of the Fall, God says Adam and Eve *shall eat the* plants *of the field*.

In Genesis 6:21, God tells Noah over 16 centuries later, to take for himself: *every sort of food that is eaten, and store it up. It shall serve as food for you and for them* (the animals). God removed the Levitical animal dietary restrictions, still followed today by some religions, in Peter's vision, described in Acts 10: 9-15 and Acts 11: 7-9, when God told Peter to: *kill and eat* and *what God has made clean, do not call common.*

In Genesis 8: 21-22, God covenanted that as long as: *the earth remains, seedtime and harvest, cold and heat, summer and winter, and day and night shall not cease.* So we see that God's supernatural protection and oversight, rather than "nature", is responsible for the continuation of our sustenance and the conservation of our necessary resources (Isaiah 46: 9-11, Acts 14: 15-17). This covenant seems to be contingent on our obedience to His statutes (Leviticus 26: 3-5, 20), which is now possible through the sacrifice of the Son of God.

One fascinating truth we can realize through a study of God's Creation is that He has programmed living creatures, and not nature, with the ability to adapt. This allows His creatures to: *be fruitful and multiply, and fill the earth* (Genesis 1:28, see also Genesis 1:22, 8: 17, 9:1,7).

Not until Genesis 9:2, after the flood, does God give all animals into the hand of man for food, and Genesis 9:3 says: *Every moving thing that lives shall be food for you. And as I gave you the green plants, I give you everything.* Even in Jesus' bodily resurrection, He ate fish, (Luke 24: 42). But God still requires us to respect and maintain the integrity of the environment. In Deuteronomy 22:6-7, He tells the Israelites tha:t *"If you come across a bird's nest in any tree or on the ground, with young ones or eggs, and the mother sitting on the young or on the eggs, you shall not take the mother with the young. You shall let the mother go, but the young you may take for yourself, that it may be well with you., and that you may live long.* God did not tell us that we cannot capture or kill animals for food or sport, but he did require us to do so in a way that preserves the species for future generations.

The Difference is Blood

Biblically, it appears that the true differentiation between plants and animals is the presence of blood. Scientifically, the difference is that animals, unlike plants, have a capacity for spontaneous movement and a rapid motor response to stimulation (Webster's New Collegiate Dictionary, 9th edition). Webster's defines *blood* as the fluid that circulates in the heart, arteries, capillaries and veins of a vertebrate animal, or the comparable fluid of an invertebrate.

In Genesis 9:4, God tells Noah that he shall not eat flesh with its *life*, that is its *blood*. Verse 6 introduces the Biblical principle that: *Whoever sheds the blood of man, by man shall his blood be shed, for God made man in* His *own image* (see also Genesis 1:27, Genesis 5:1).

God has said that to murder a human being is to murder what is most like God, and is therefore an attack directly on God. Leviticus 17:11 says the *life*, or *soul* of the flesh is in the blood and Leviticus 17:14 says: *for the life* (or soul) *of every creature is its blood: its blood is its life*.

Deuteronomy 12:23 says: *Only be sure that you do not eat the blood, for the blood is the life* (soul), *and you shall not eat the life* (soul) *with the flesh*. Indeed, we as Christians are" *freed from our sins by Jesus' blood*" (Revelation 1:5, Ephesians 1:7, 2:23,

Hebrews 13:12, I John 1:7). It is logical that since Jesus' blood has saved us, then its symbolism in differentiating us from evolutionary beginnings without blood is significant.

So God created us from dust (inorganics), with His breath, as His temple, as unique beings with blood, a soul, a spirit and a mind, with the purpose of loving Him and serving Him by having dominion over His Creation.

Chapter 7

The Rise, Fall and Re-Creation of the Environment

The Rise and Fall in the Old World

In the first two chapters of the Bible, God has given us several critical directions for our relation to the environment:

- God created the earth, the sky, the sun, the moon and the rest of the universe for mankind's benefit.
- God created vegetation for the sustenance of man and animals and differentiated man and vegetation.
- God later allowed meat for the sustenance of man and animals.

- God gave man dominion and responsibility over animals and differentiated between man and animals.
- God charged man to tend and keep the Garden and the soil.

As seen above, the truth of God's creation is not limited to the book of Genesis. The writer of Hebrews even states that the first test of faith is the understanding: *that the universe was created by the Word of God, so that what is seen was not made out of things which that are visible* (Hebrews 11:3).

An insistence on only believing natural science (the seen), indeed limits, or can even destroy, our faith: *without faith it is impossible to please* Him (Hebrews 11:6). 2 Peter 3:4b-6 says: *all things are continuing as they were from the beginning of* Creation. *For they deliberately overlook this fact, that the heavens existed long ago and the earth was formed out of water and through water by the* Word *of God, and that by means of these the world that then existed was deluged with water and perished.*

We potentially can affect the environment as far as the health of ourselves, animals and vegetation, but we can't really change the natural weather and geological disasters that we experience as a result of the Fall.

Our efforts cannot make the environment on earth radically better, or worse, but they can make the environment on this earth more pleasant and less dangerous for us and for our children.

God has promised that He will hold the environment together and uphold the universe with His power. Colossians 1:17: *And* He *is before all things, and in* Him *all things hold together.* Hebrews 1:3: *He* (Jesus) *is the radiance of the glory of God and the exact imprint of* His *nature, and* He *holds up the universe by the word of* His *power.* With this assurance and His power, we, as His stewards are not without unlimited resources to complete our mandate for protecting our environment.

The Re-Creation of the New World

The Need for a New World

We have seen so far in this book that man has a Biblical responsibility to protect and improve our environment, but that because of the fall of man resulting in the curse of God and the decay of the environment, the complete recovery is impossible without the intervention of our Creator.

Romans 8: 20-22 tells us that: *For the* Creation *was subjected to futility, not willingly, but because of* Him *who subjected it, in hope that the* Creation *itself will be set free from its bondage to decay and obtain the freedom of the glory of the children of God. For we know that the whole* Creation *has been groaning together in the pains of childbirth until now"*.

So the Bible tells us that God sees forward to a time when nature is set free from the results of human sin so that it will no longer be caught in the pains of childbirth and will allow the final freedom of the children of God. The *decay* in verse 21 above is a description of our scientific law of entropy; *the degradation of the matter and the energy in the universe to an ultimate state of inert uniformity(1).* Entropy is one of the basic scientific arguments against evolution.

We must ask why the environment is in a position so that it has to be destroyed and replaced. As we have seen previously in Genesis 1 and 2, the environment was created good. Eve and Adam were tempted by an animal (a serpent) to eat vegetation (from the tree of the knowledge of good and evil), which they did since it was:

- Good for food
- A delight to the eyes
- Desirable to make them wise

These words from Genesis 3:6 make it clear that Adam and Eve were tempted by the same tempter who tempts us today, to commit the same three basic sins as expressed in Exodus 20: 3-17 in the Ten Commandments, that we commit today;

- greed (Commandments 5,6,7 and 8),
- lust (Commandments 9 and 10), and
- God envy (Commandments 1,2,3 and 4).

All of this started as a lie from Satan (Genesis 3:4 *But the serpent said to the woman, 'You will not surely die. For God knows that when you eat of it your eyes will be opened and you will be like God,*

---

(1) *Webster's Ninth New Collegiate Dictionary*

knowing good and evil', and resulted in a lie from Eve and Adam to themselves (Genesis 3:6:*So when the woman saw that the tree was good for food, and that it was a delight to the eyes, and that the tree was to be desired to make one wise, she took of its fruit and ate, and she also gave some to her husband who was with her, and he ate)*. This sin of wanting to be God was so grievous to God, that He did not even finish the sentence in Genesis 3,verse 22: *Then the Lord God said 'Behold, the man has become like one of us in knowing good and evil. Now, lest he reach out his hand and take also of the tree of life and eat, and live forever-'*. For man to live forever in a sinful condition was an unbearable thought and God must waste no time to prevent it, so he sent Adam and Eve out of the Garden. Instead of man's priestly duty to guard and care for the garden, he was removed outside to work the ground. The priestly duty reverted to the cherubim and a flaming sword to guard the garden and the tree of life (Genesis 3:24).

All humans are tempted to sin for something that satisfies our greedy wants, that appeals to our lusts, or that gives us the knowledge of good and evil. These temptations are still, and always will be our failing, especially the temptation to be God, which is the root of all evil.

Without the grace of God, the payment of Jesus, and the power of the Holy Spirit, we are completely inadequate to resist these temptations. The Word of God in the Bible and the presence of His Spirit within us, guard us from our temptation to want to be God (Ephesians 6:17: *and take the helmet of salvation, and the sword of the Spirit which is the* Word *of God, praying at all times in the Spirit, with all prayer and supplication.*, Hebrews 4:12).

As a result of our ancestor's sin, God cursed the serpent, (Genesis 3:14b; *cursed are you above all livestock and above all beasts of the field*); gave pain in childbirth and submission of the woman to the man, (Genesis 3:16: *To the woman* He *said, 'I will surely multiply your pain in childbearing; in pain you shall bring forth children. Your desire shall be for your husband, and he shall rule over you'*); and cursed the ground, (Genesis 3:17: *And to Adam* He *said 'Because you have listened to the voice of your wife and have eaten of the tree of which I commanded you, 'You shall not eat of it', cursed is the ground because of you; in pain you shall eat of it all the days of your life', also Genesis* 5:25) because of Adam; and required that he toil for his food; and introduced sweat and death, (3:19: *By the sweat of your face you shall eat bread, till you return to the ground*).

He returned us to dust, and death came into the world for the first time (Genesis 2:17, 3:19, 1 Corinthians:15: 21,22, Romans 5:12, 15-17). *Sweat* is mentioned in the Bible only two other times, as a curse that God's servants had to be separated from in Ezekiel 44:18 (Jude 23), and in Jesus' agony in prayer before his crucifixion in the garden of Gethsemane in Luke 22:44, when His *sweat* became like drops of blood. Jesus' blood substituted for the curse in the Garden, but the result of the curse remains in the old world until the new heavens and earth are formed.

Romans 8:20-22 tells us that the Creation longs and waits for the revealing of the sons of God: *For the* Creation *was subjected to futility* because of God (8:20), Who *subjected it, in hope that the* Creation *itself will be set free from its bondage to decay and obtain the freedom of the glory of the children of God.*

Therefore the effects of the Fall are:

- Man against God
- Man against man
- Man against nature
- Nature against man
- Man against himself

When we are set free from the curse in the new world, our relation to the new environment in Heaven is described to some extent in the Bible.

Our Environment In the New World

The verses below describe the extent of this freedom from the curse so that humans in Heaven will at last live in harmony with the environment.

Isaiah 65:17 says: *For behold I create new heavens and a new earth* (see also Isaiah 66:22), *and the former things shall not be remembered or come to mind.*

Isaiah 65:20-24 says that: *No more shall there be in it an infant who lives but a few days, or an old man who does not fill out his days; for the young man shall die a hundred years old, and the sinner a hundred years old shall be accursed. They shall build houses and inhabit them; they shall plant vineyards and eat their fruit. They shall not build and another inhabit; they shall not plant and another eat; for like the days of a tree, shall the days of my people be; and my chosen shall long enjoy the work of their hands. They shall not labor in vain or bear children for calamity, for they shall be the offspring of the blessed of the Lord, they and their descendents with them.*

The curse of death is removed by Jesus and everyone will live forever in a paradise with houses, vineyards, fruit and other plants.

In Isaiah 11:6-8, God tells us: *The wolf shall dwell with the lamb, and the leopard shall lie down with the young goat, and the calf and the lion and the fattened calf together* (or will feed together*); and a little child shall lead them. The cow and the bear shall graze; their young shall lie down together; and the lion shall eat straw like the ox. The nursing child shall play over the hole of the cobra, and the weaned child shall put his hand on the adder's den.*

Isaiah 65:25: The *wolf and the lamb shall graze together, and the lion shall eat straw like the ox.*

This new heaven and earth will not only give us a pure relationship to the non -human part of our environment, but also to ourselves and other souls in Heaven.

Job 33: 23-28 tells us that because of our ransom by Jesus, our soul will be delivered from the pit in righteousness and our flesh will become fresh with youth and we will return to our days of youthful vigor.

2 Peter 3:13 says: *But according to His promise we are waiting for new heavens and a new earth in which righteousness dwells.*

No More Death

Isaiah 25:8 tells us that: *He will swallow up death forever; and the Lord God will wipe away tears from all faces, and the reproach of* His *people* He *will take away from all the earth, for the Lord has spoken.* Part of this verse is quoted by Paul in 1 Corinthians 15: 54, followed by verse 57 which says: *But thanks be to God* Who *gives us the victory through our Lord Jesus Christ.*

I Corinthians 15:26 says: *The last enemy to be destroyed is death.* Revelation 21:4 says: *He will wipe away every tear from their eyes, and death shall be no more, neither shall there be mourning, nor crying, nor pain anymore, for the former things have passed away.* Jesus' death and resurrection have defeated death. As 1 Corinthians 15:44 says: *It is sown a natural body; it is raised a spiritual body. If there is a natural body there is also a spiritual body.* Our bodies will be raised imperishable. 1 Corinthians 15: 42 says: *So it is with the resurrection of the dead. What is sown is perishable; what is raised is imperishable.* 1 Corinthians 15: 52-54 repeats this promise.

The New Heaven and the New Earth

God in His grace has elected to tell us certain things about Heaven in parables and through prophets and through John's visions. Revelation 21:1b says that when the: *first heaven and the first earth had passed away, and the sea was no more.* This promise apparently refers to earthly rebellion, chaos and danger (the sea of the beast of Revelation 13;1 which will no longer be present). Revelation 22:1-2 speaks of the river of the water of life flowing through the middle of the street of the city; the water of the new Heaven.

In Heaven we will finally dwell with God (Revelation 21:3). As His people, we will enjoy Heaven's radiance: *like a most rare jewel, like a jasper, clear as crystal* (Revelation 21:11, see also Revelation 21: 18-21); the beauty of inorganics in Heaven.

Revelation 21;23 says: *And the City has no need for sun or moon to shine on it, for the glory of God gives it light, and its lamp is the lamb*. Isaiah 60: 19:20 also prophesizes as does Revelation 22:5.

The river of the water of life, described in Revelation 22: 1-2 will water the *tree of life* with its twelve kinds (or crops) of fruit, yielding its fruit each month.

So, we will enjoy the beauty of organic plants, along with the beauty of inorganic gems. Interestingly, Revelation 22 verse 2b says that: *The leaves of the tree were for the healing of the nations*, presumably because of the destruction of death. Vegetation, which originally provided sustenance for humans and animals, will in the New Heaven, be used for the sustenance of the nations.

Revelation 22:14 says that we will have the right to the tree of life (the tree of the knowledge of good and evil of Genesis 2:17, 3:22). No longer will the knowledge of good and evil be kept from us.

The Survival of Organics and Inorganics

We have seen that the inorganic creation of water from Genesis 1:1-7 survives as the river of the water of life of Revelation 22:1-2, clear as crystal from the throne of God and the Lamb. Jesus promised this in John 4:10-14. 7:38-39 and Isaiah 44:3.

The inorganic creation of minerals from Genesis 1:2 survives as the minerals, precious and semi precious jewels. The twelve jewels adorning the city's apostolic foundations (Revelation 21: 19-20), correspond to the twelve Israeli tribe symbols on the breastplates of the high priest described in Exodus 28: 17-20. These stones are also similar to those described by Ezekiel in 28:12-19 as having been in the Garden of Eden anointing the fallen angel Satan, and God will use them as a permanent reminder in Heaven of the futility of the corruption of evil and reclaim their beauty for His children.

Vegetation, created as described in Genesis 1: 11-12, survives as new vineyards and fruit trees (Revelation 22:1-2).

Animals survive as seen above as new wolves, lambs, lions, oxen, leopards, kids, calves, cows, bears, cobras and vipers; both wild and domestic animals.

Humans survive as new nursing children, weaned children, little boys, men and women (Isaiah:11:6-8, Mark 12:25), with no sickness or infirmities.

The old organics, vegetables, animals and humans that have died return to dust through death so that they do not survive as organics. They instead are transformed by God through Jesus' blood into a new life as new souls in the new Heaven and new earth.

But the sun and the moon do not survive; there is no reason (Genesis 1: 14-18). God said that the purpose of the astronomical existence was to:

- Separate day and night (Genesis 1:14)
- Act as signs (1:14)
- For seasons (1:14)
- For days and years (1:14)
- To give light (1:15)
- To govern the day and night (1:16)

But God replaces these purposes in Revelation 21 and 22 ". . .for the Lord God will be their light". There will be no need for day and night, for signs, seasons, days and years.

Praise God!

Chapter 8

Science Speaks Out About the Environment

ack in the late 1970's, I was called to be an officer and a Sunday School teacher in my church. The spiritual growth I experienced during this period of my life closely followed my graduate education in environmental engineering. I have always believed that God used this combination of circumstances to help me understand to a limited extent, some of the wonders of His Creation and how the sciences of geology, hydrology, hydraulics, biology, microbiology, biochemistry, archeology, anthropology and astronomy, all confirm the teaching of the Bible.

So, through God's opening and closing doors for me, I have become a Christian environmentalist. As such, I have a strong belief that each of us, once God leads us to Himself, has an obligation to also be a Christian environmentalist. The Bible teaches us this, and contrary to secular teaching, so does science. The purpose of this chapter and Chapter 5 is to introduce this concept and discuss our response.

The challenge of being a Christian environmentalist is related to the fact that with time, our environment does and will continue to change. This change in the environment is caused by nature itself, or by human activities affecting nature. Our stewardship of the environment does not extend to the actions of nature which are not affected by our activities, such as solar activity, el Niño and la Niña effects. We can respond to these natural actions through repair and rebuilding, and we can protect ourselves from some natural disasters, but we cannot control them. The Genesis 1:28 mandate for us to subdue the earth and rule over its living things does not seem to include natural weather effects, at least under current technology.

Historically, weather has had major effects, some positive and some negative, on living organisms. Over time, as a result, some organisms have become extinct, others have adapted or micro-evolved within their kinds, and continue to exist. This fact leads us to believe that the power to solve natural and human caused environmental challenges resides in the organisms and not the environment. Logically, nature has no mind or power to change existing organisms to adapt to its weather related changes, but God has programmed organisms through His mind with this power of adaptability (Isaiah 46: 9b,10: *I am God, and there is none like* Me; *declaring the end from the beginning and from ancient times things not yet done, saying 'My counsel shall stand and I will accomplish all* My *purpose';* Ephesians 1: 9-10: *making known to us the mystery of* His *will, according to* His *purpose, which* He *set forth in Christ, as a plan for the fullness of time, to unite all things in* Him, *things in Heaven and things on earth.*

It is also logical that if this ability resides in organisms for naturally caused adaption, it can also function in human caused changes. But as stewards, it is our job to minimize environmental changes so that organism disruptions are limited. Contrary to current thought, all types of vegetation and animal organisms need not be preserved forever.

Like some humans, some organisms are disruptive to others and the Darwinian Theory of survival of the fittest, rather than human activity, tends to control their extinction and micro-evolution.

In addition to our inability to control the weather effects on the environment, certain chemicals which exist naturally can damage the environment, including the health of humans, especially in large concentrations. These include inorganic particulates such as wind blown dust and sand, inorganic metals such as lead and mercury, and organics such as natural gas and coal. Many of these naturally occurring chemicals are difficult or impossible to control or neutralize.

But God in his wisdom has created a universe that is adaptable and correcting to self damage so that recovery with time has always occurred. The advancement of civilization has allowed us to combine these natural elements and compounds to develop many synthetic compounds that can help, but also potentially harm the environment. We have found that virtually all of these damaging synthetic compounds can be broken apart if we understand their manufacturing process. This is the challenge of science and engineering.

Science and Engineering are Different

The study of the environment is *science* and the use of science to protect and improve the environment is *engineering*.

The environment consists of metallic and non-metallic elements and molecules and organic and inorganic molecules. These elements and molecules consist of atomic and sub atomic particles that are a wonderful universe unto themselves. Science is daily understanding more about this sub atomic universe, and with this knowledge, is more able to understand the actual and potential relationships between these particles. Science and engineering combine to use this knowledge to develop new compounds which can either help or harm the environment.

Ideally, each time a new compound is synthesized, a method is developed to assure that the by products and disposal of the compound will not negatively effect the environment. Unfortunately, there are minimal enforcement mechanisms, or moral or even financial incentives available to encourage this life cycle approach to sustainable growth. Therefore society is continuously searching for ways to control and treat the residuals of civilization. The purpose of environmental engineering is to develop practices and projects to prevent deterioration of our environment and to aid in its improvement.

Scientific and engineering advances to date have been very encouraging. Air and water pollution control have made great strides toward a sustainable level, but much work remains to be accomplished to make our atmosphere truly sustainable in its capacity to accommodate the discharge of residuals from the future growth of civilization.

Land pollution control has not realized the improvement of air and water, perhaps because it is difficult to access and control. Unknown acreage, probably in the millions, in the United States contains pollution from the past, when rules were non existent or lax, and most residual discharge was transferred to the ground, either as fall-out from the air, or water pollution, or as a direct application. Indeed, the ground can be said to be the final resting place of pollution and the most difficult to treat toward recovery.

The relationship between scientists and engineers is that scientists perform research and propose scientific theories, which if proven true through the Scientific Method, become laws of science. Engineers implement these laws and develop projects to benefit mankind. Hence the term research and development, describes the activities of a team of scientists and engineers dedicated to practically solving social challenges.

The Limitations of Science

One should exercise caution in only relying on the scientific response to environmental issues since that response is subsidiary to the Biblical response. It is impossible for a scientist, regardless of their experience to have the mind of God. God created science and has allowed man to discover a small amount of scientific truth in order to implement his mandate of exercising dominion over the earth.

Not only are scientists limited in their understanding of the environment by their mental capacity, but they are typically trained and have expertise in just a few disciplines. The environment consists of all disciplines and no one is practically capable of becoming an expert in every one.

Another limitation of science is that it, as commonly practiced, is limited to natural science. Since the beginning of the universe in Creation is spiritual in nature, science is unable to understand or discover the source of the beginning. It is impossible for a scientist to accurately explain the mix of elements necessary to begin this universe, or cause the Big Bang to occur. Science must say that these elements always existed, which without a spiritual acceptance cannot be justified, or say that the elements appeared from nothing, which proves a God. Science further has been unable to explain the construction of these primal elements, even with the energy of the Big Bang, into the DNA and RNA required for life. Without a supernatural God, science is powerless to explain reality before man's observation, and is powerless to explain the supernatural.

Science has developed rules for scientific laws and theories. For a theory to become a law, its results must meet a threefold test; be originally observed, be documented, and be able to be repeated by other scientists. Scientists tend to accept theories that they have learned and agree with, as laws.

An example is the ever evolving Theory of Evolution. Much incorrect scientific information has been published and later determined incorrect, because of the pre-conceived notion of certain elements of evolutionary theory. The saddest example of this is the acceptance by theologians of some modification of evolution, which causes them to not accept Genesis1-3 and 6-9 as history. For instance the *Literary Framework* view of these chapters of God's Word *portrays the Creation week as if it were a workweek, but without concern for temporal sequence*(1).

The danger of this error is found in the first sentence of that paragraph which states *The relation of Genesis to science is primarily a question of how one reads the accounts of creation and the fall (Chapters 1-3) and of the flood (Chapters 6-9)*. This statement, if completely honest, should read *The relation of science to Genesis is completely a question of how God describes the Fall and the flood*. We do not have the right to interpret a Biblical book of history as a myth, poetry, a literary manipulation, a mistake by God, or even esoteric and confusing words interpretable only by theologians.

In any of these cases God would be failing in His communication with His children, and the rest of His Word must also be taken as interpreted by science

---

(1) *English Standard Version Study Bible, Introduction to Genesis, Genesis and Science).*

only. Before we fall into this trap, we must ask whether science is our god or not (See Romans 1: 20-22: *For His invisible attributes, namely His eternal power and divine nature, have been clearly perceived, ever since the creation of the world, in the things that have been made. So they are without excuse. For although they knew God, they did not honor Him as God, or give thanks to Him, but they became futile in their thinking, and their foolish hearts were darkened. Claiming to be wise, they became fools.*, 2 Peter 3:16: *as he* (Paul) *does in all his letters, when he speaks in them of these matters. There are some things in them therefore hard to understand, which the ignorant and unstable twist to their own destruction, as they do the other Scriptures.*)

A challenge to a Christian Environmentalist that tests the limitations of science is a grasp of a complete understanding of each specific part of the environment, whether it be a molecule of DNA, or the Mississippi River Basin. That grasp must include an answer to the question of how that part of the environment came to be, how it now exists, and how it functions in and responds to the rest of the environment. A much debated sub-set of this challenge is *does a specific part of the environment exist as it is because of the pressures by the environment, or is the specific part of the environment able to react and respond to the rest of the environment in order to change into something that can exist as it now is?*

The *evolutionary* side of this controversy will answer the question that specific parts of the environment have adapted through survival of the fittest, to changing pressures by the environment. In other words, the environment causes specific parts of itself to change and evolve into different parts, better able to survive (environmental adaptability).

The *creation* side of the controversy will answer that God created specific parts of the environment with the capability to adapt to changing pressures by the environment. In other words, the environment changes and the specific parts remain basically the same, but adapt to environmental changes (creator engineered adaptability).

Having explored the strengths and limitations of science, the rest of this chapter introduces the opportunities we have through science and engineering to control our pollution.

The following sections should introduce the reader to typical air, wastewater and land treatment practices and demonstrate the practicality, feasibility and limitations of this treatment. In my opinion, there is no objective reason for our civilization not to be able to afford the construction of facilities adequate for removing pollutants and preventing pollution to a level which will protect our health and environment and allow sustainable growth.

Our Challenge to Clean up the Air

The willingness and awareness of our governments has resulted in environmental regulations that have returned the air in most U.S. cities to a much cleaner condition than existed before the 1960's. Advances in science have enabled engineers to determine the source of polluting air emissions and design treatment systems to remove pollution to an acceptable level.

From a regulatory perspective in the air, pollutants generally fall into solids, mists and vapors which typically either flow through a vent or stack, as a direct source, or through miscellaneous points and areas, as fugitive emissions. In order to control these emissions, they must be first characterized as to their quantity and quality.

Air Source Testing

Direct source emissions, since they are emitted from a vent or stack can be measured by inserting several tubes or probes into a stack at a point and in a manner such that the velocity, temperature and pollutant concentration can be measured. The pollutants can be caught for measurement in similar ways to those described below which are used for treatment to remove the pollutants.

These captured pollutants are tested to determine their concentration, and in the case of solids, their size and size distribution. With that concentration and the air velocity and temperature leaving the stack, the total weight of pollutants per time period can be calculated and reported.

Air Emissions Modeling

When the pollutants have been characterized, mathematical models, or formulae, can be used to predict the amount and direction of pollutant distribution from the source. There are so many variables affecting these calculations that it is difficult to develop a model which is very accurate.

Some *successful* models may only yield answers within plus or minus fifty percent of the actual pollutant concentration at some point downwind of a stack. This is largely because of the inaccuracy of wind direction and velocity predictions. But other interferences such as atmospheric conditions, hills and buildings will affect the results of the prediction.

Air Pollutants

The EPA has, in the Clean Air Act of 1972, listed five main classes of air pollutants; particulate matter, sulfur dioxide, carbon monoxide, nitrogen oxides and hydrocarbons. Lead was added to this list in 1976.

Particulate matter is any finely divided solid or liquid material, other than uncombined water. Particulate matter causes decreased visibility in air, smoke and dust affect on human health, chronic respiratory disease, asbestosis, lead poisoning, destruction of plant life and affects on climate.

Sulfur dioxides (SO_2) are acid, corrosive, poisonous gases, produced when fuel containing sulfur is burned. SO_2 in the air is a cause of acid rain and causes breathing difficulty, coughing, and mucous secretion and can destroy plant life and fish.

Carbon monoxide (CO) is a colorless, odorless, poisonous gas, produced by the incomplete combustion of carbon in fuels. CO can be fatal in a short time through its prevention of oxygen transfer in the blood.

Nitrogen oxides (NOx) are colorless gases with excessive concentrations in air having a brownish color due to light absorption in the blue-green area of the spectrum. NOx is produced by burning fuel at very high temperatures, from nitrogen in the air, and from organic nitrogen in coal and heavy oils. NOx causes reduced visibility in air, nose and eye irritation, pulmonary edema, bronchitis and pneumonia. NOx also reacts with volatile organic compounds under the influence of sunlight to form ozone and smog, which cause severe eye, nose and throat irritation and damage plant life.

Hydrocarbons are classified into VOCs (volatile organic compounds) and Non-VOCs and include any compound of carbon except carbon monoxide, carbon dioxide, carbonic acid, metallic carbides, ammonium carbonate and acetone, which precipitate in atmospheric photochemical reactions. EPA also lists some light chloro-fluoro and heavy compounds as Non-VOCs. VOCs are the primary pollutants in the formation of ozone and smog. Non-VOCs are stratospheric ozone depleters. The ozone layer of the stratosphere protects the earth from excessive ultraviolent radiation.

Lead is a heavy metal which can attack the central nervous system, with subsequent neurological damage. It is chronic and accumulates in the body organs.

Note: These EPA Criteria Pollutant descriptions are taken from *"Air Quality Control Handbook"*, by E. Roberts Alley & Associates, Inc., McGraw-Hill, 1998.

As explained in Chapter 2, the 1990 Clean Air Act Amendments also regulate mobile sources, hazardous air pollutants, acid rain and ozone depleting chemicals.

Air Pollution Control Methods

Solids in a source discharge, called particulates, can be removed by settling, inertial separation, filtering and impacting. The ability to remove particulates using one or more of these methods depends on the characterization of the solid, primarily its size, charge, density and chemistry.

Settling is accomplished by lowering the velocity of the solid sufficiently to allow it to settle. These settled solids must be removed without affecting the efficiency of the settling. The practical difficulty of settling in an air stream is the cost of constructing an air chamber large enough to cause particulates to settle. But these chambers are still the simplest devices for removing particulates.

Inertial separators separate particulates from the air because of their different densities by increasing the force of gravity, normally using cyclone centrifugal equipment.

Filtering is accomplished by straining, with openings sized according to the diameter of the particulates. The filtering efficiency can be increased by electrically charging the filter surface. The filtered solids must be removed by shaking, air pulsing or washing. Examples of air filters are those on home heating and air conditioning units and industrial bag houses.

Impacting is accomplished by placing a solid shape across the path of air flow, which causes the particulate to impact the solid shape. A screen is a simple impactor. More complex shapes use Bernoulli's Law to accelerate the tendency to impact.

Mists and vapors or gases in an air stream can be removed by absorption, adsorption, incineration, bio-filtration or condensation. Mists are small droplets of liquid which are conveyed out of a source discharge by the velocity of the air flow. These mists may be in the form of acids, such as hydrochloric acid (HCl), organics such as benzene or heavy metals absorbed in liquid. The EPA defines mists as particulates since most removal mechanisms are similar.

Vapors are molecules of chemicals which have evaporated from liquids and are carried by air velocity from a source. Vapors must be chemically altered in order to be removed by a physical method.

Absorption uses a compatible liquid solvent, usually water, in a mist or spray form to absorb particulates by allowing the mist or vapor to come in contact with tiny liquid droplets. One purpose of absorbing an air pollutant is to convert it into a water pollutant that may be less expensive or more efficient to remove.

Adsorption is accomplished by allowing the air stream to come in contact with a solid shape, such as granular activated carbon, activated alumina, molecular sieves, silica gel or resins. The act of adsorbing effectively changes an air pollutant to a solid pollutant. The solid depleted adsorbent must be cleaned or replaced, resulting in a liquid or solid waste.

Incineration is the rapid oxidation of VOCs in an air stream. In order to break down an organics into CO_2, water and inorganic residuals if they exist, the temperature must reach 1000 to 1500oF. This treatment is very expensive and must have a special permit to operate, but will result in high removals of organics.

Biofiltration is the use of microorganisms in a chamber to biologically degrade or oxidize organic air pollutants into CO_2 and water. This method requires that the media on which the bacteria grow, which can be leaves or saw dust, is kept moist and warm and supplied with certain nutrients.

Condensation is a phase change from gas to liquid, basically, the opposite of boiling. The advantage of this cooling process is that certain gases can be re-used.

The particulates or liquids removed from air must be recycled or disposed of as *residuals*. This is an example of a gaseous waste being converted into a liquid or solid waste.

Carbon Dioxide Control

Industrialization of our society has caused a continuing increase in the concentration of CO_2 in the atmosphere. The EPA has listed CO_2 as a Green House Gas (ghg) which can contribute to the greenhouse effect by limiting back radiation of light coming to the earth. Many other ghgs have been eliminated or reduced by regulations, but CO_2 is the natural emission from animal breathing and the product of combustion, and as such is much more difficult to control. There are four general methods of reducing or eliminating the CO_2 increase in the atmosphere:

- Minimize combustion by substituting alternative energy production sources such as nuclear, hydrogen, wind, solar, geothermal, and hydraulic (waves and stream flow).
- Use renewable carbon sources such as methane, wood and vegetation (biomass) instead of non-renewable sources such as coal, gas and oil. Even though the amount of CO_2 added to the atmosphere is roughly the same, renewable sources not combusted will eventually emit CO_2 upon decomposition if not harvested, where non-renewable sources add net CO_2 to the atmosphere for the first time when they are burned, rather than recycling CO_2 that is already in the carbon cycle. Therefore, there is a net CO_2 increase in the atmosphere only from non-renewable sources.
- Increase the efficiency of combustion so that less CO_2 is emitted relative to organics destroyed.
- Capture and secure by sequestering the CO_2 emissions in water, soil or vegetation. The CO_2 is captured and stored (not destroyed or used) in water and soil (even deep injection)

and beneficially used only by vegetation. These sequestering reservoirs are called sinks.

According to *Carbon Sequestering* (1), the following sources and sinks are annual estimates of the global CO2 cycle during the 1990s:

CO2 Source	GtC*	CO2 Sink	GtC*
Human and animal respiration	60.0	Vegetation (photosynthesis)	61.7
Deforestation	1.4	None	0
Fossil fuels	6.0	None	0
Decay of ocean vegetation	90.0	Ocean Uptake	92.2
Source total	157.4	Sink total	153.9

* Billion metric tons of carbon from CO2= gigatons carbon (GtC)

These estimates indicate that an estimated 3.5 GtC per year enters and remains in the atmosphere.

Recent research attempts to quantify the loss and gain of CO2 in the ocean due to temperature variation, but these estimates are difficult to substantiate because of the variability of ocean temperatures due to geography, seasons and currents.

The ocean is estimated to contain about 40,000 GtC of CO2.

---

(1) An on-line course by Lee Layton, based on the U.S. Department of Energy report *Carbon Sequestration Research and Development*, December, 1999

If vegetative sequestration remains the same, the oceans would only increase CO2 by 8.75% in 1,000 years, but because of the logarithmic nature of pH, there could be a gradual lowering of ocean pH caused by human activities (deforestation and fossil fuels) which could affect the growth of coral reefs in an area contaminated with acid, and consequently, a loss of local ocean biomass.

The vegetation sink for CO2 has a potential through management policies to affect the sequestration of human caused CO2 emissions. Because of the increase in vegetative growth in the United States in recent years, there is a trend of net increase of CO2 sequestered; but in the entire world in 2000, there has been a net annual reduction of CO2 sequestration twenty times larger than the U.S. increase (1).

EPA has estimated that through changes in agricultural soil and forest management, tree planting and biofuel substitution, the U.S. could increase its vegetative sequestration by 30 to 90%. In 2002, about 12% of the total CO2 emitted in the U.S was sequestered.

It should be emphasized that young forests use more CO2 per acre than old forests. Young trees, like teenagers, metabolize more rapidly, using more CO2, and old forests have more products of decay which produce CO2. It has been estimated that a tree takes up about 2.52 pounds of CO2 per day (2). This

---

(1) *Trend Estimates of Land-Use Sequestration*, U.S. EPA

(2) *Tufts Climate Initiative, "Sequestration: How much CO2 does a tree take up?*

means that roughly one 25 year old tree is required to take up CO_2 exhaled by an average man (1).

Air Regulatory Compliance

The EPA has established Rules and Regulations which set standards for pollutant discharges as discussed in Chapter 2. These standards result in the issuance of air permits to dischargers. In order to meet these established standards, the air permits allow dischargers of air pollutants to construct and operate treatment systems.

Once a system has been designed and installed to remove pollutants, the discharger must assure permit compliance by periodically testing the source emissions, or in lieu of testing, measure and/or record a treatment parameter such as pressure or quality of fuel.

Our Challenge to Clean up the Water

As described above in *Air Pollution Control*, solids, liquid chemicals and gases must be removed from the air at the source of discharge in order to allow the air to retain its natural quality. Likewise, in water pollution control, solids, liquid chemicals and dissolved chemicals must be removed from the water in order to prevent its degradation.

The general engineering approach in each case is similar; solids in water can be removed through

---

(1) Wikipedia, *Carbon Dioxide*

screening, filtering, settling, flotation or evaporation; and dissolved organic chemicals in water can be removed or neutralized through chemical treatment, biological treatment, coagulation, flocculation, settling (after the dissolved organics have been converted to colloids and solids), incineration and/or adsorption. Inorganic dissolved chemicals in water can be removed or neutralized through chemical treatment, coagulation, flocculation (after conversion to colloids), precipitation, stripping and/or concentration. In order to determine the most efficient and feasible means of treatment, the water is first tested and characterized.

Physical Treatment of Wastewater

The purpose of physical treatment of wastewater is to relatively inexpensively remove undissoved solids before further chemical or biological treatment, to settle solids formed during chemical or biological treatment, or to evaporate the water, thereby concentrating solids for recycle or disposal.

One of the simplest and most basic characteristics of wastewater is the differentiation between dissolved and undissolved solids. For testing and enforcement purposes, this differentiation is made by filtering the sample through a glass fiber filter. The solids caught on the filter are weighed and reported as Total Suspended Solids. The liquid passing through the filter is evaporated, the residue weighed, and reported as Total Dissolved Solids.

A second basic wastewater test is to allow a liter of wastewater to settle and float for 30 minutes and measure the volume of the sediment or float. This ratio of sediment to wastewater by volume is called Settleable Solids. In a Settleable Solids test, the solid settling or floating velocity can be measured and this rate converted into the size basin required for settling or floating of a solid or liquid of that size and density.

When there is a variable size and density of particles or droplets, the basin size will be that required for the minimum sized particle or droplet that will allow the discharge permit to be met. When needed, solid sizes can be measured by screening, and the temperature of the discharged wastewater determined. An additional value of interest is the variability of the wastewater flow and pollutant concentration, because treatment facilities must be designed for peak conditions.

The analysis of these relatively simple tests will allow an engineer to size screening, settling, and filtering systems that can lower inorganic and some non- dissolved organic solids to an acceptable level.

Screens consist of a solid grid sized to remove solids larger than the grid size.

Settling is accomplished in basins sized for the settling velocity of the smallest and/or least dense particle to be removed. These basins must be relatively quiescent and may have mechanical float and or sediment removal equipment, but may be simple ponds.

Evaporation is a solid/ liquid concentration method which is efficient but very energy intensive.

Screened, floated, and settled solids and the solid *residuals* from evaporation are typically recycled or sent to a landfill. This is an example of a liquid waste being converted into a solid waste.

Chemical Treatment of Wastewater

The purpose of chemical treatment of wastewater is to use chemicals to alter the wastewater to the point where it can meet its discharge permit, or to pre treat the wastewater to prepare it for biological treatment.

The chemical characterization of wastewater is much more complex and expensive than the physical characterization since there are so many types of organic and inorganic chemicals. There are a few basic chemical tests which can aid in determining a treatment approach.

Conductivity is a measure of the dissolved solids mentioned as a physical pollutant, and is an indication of the salt content of the wastewater.

Alkalinity is a measure of the carbonate, bicarbonate and carbon dioxide in a wastewater.

Hardness is a measure of the calcium and magnesium in a wastewater.

pH is a measure of the hydrogen ions in the wastewater and tells whether the water is acidic (low pH), or basic, corrosive or scaling. By definition, pH is the negative logarithm of the hydrogen ion concentration.

Fats, Oils and Grease is a measure of the petroleum, animal and/or vegetable oils in a wastewater.

Dissolved Oxygen is a measure of the oxygen content of a water. Colder water will dissolve more oxygen than warmer water.

Other chemical tests are available for all of the organic and inorganic pollutants found in wastewater but can be expensive.

Once the wastewater is chemically characterized and its variability determined, a treatment method can be selected. The following are examples of chemical treatments that have been successful in removing pollutants to acceptable levels:

Neutralization adds acids for high pH wastewaters and bases for low pH wastewaters to reach a more neutral level. The lowest pH is zero, the highest is 14, and neutral is 7.

Some wastewaters can be *oxidized or reduced* to aid in their treatment. These are reversible chemical reactions which can change the characteristics of an inorganic waste.

Precipitation of metals is the chemical treatment used to allow the metal to change from being soluble, to insoluble so that it can be removed by settling or filtering. Most metal solubilities are pH dependent and can be more soluble at either low or high pH levels.

Coagulation is the addition of chemicals to a wastewater to destroy or reduce repulsive forces and allow the solids to agglomerate, or stick together.

Flocculation is the physical process following chemical addition to promote particle contact to facilitate agglomeration.

Disinfection is the process of inactivating all bacteria from wastewater. Sterilization is the process of inactivating all organisms. Disinfection only is normally required and consists of adding a halogen such as chlorine or bromine, a metal such as silver or copper, ozone, hydrogen peroxide, an acid, a base or a detergent to water to kill bacteria. Ultraviolet radiation can also be used for disinfection. After disinfection, some of these chemicals must be removed to prevent their being pollutants themselves.

Stripping is used to transfer a water pollutant to the air by evaporating the chemical under conditions of optimum temperature, mixing of the air and wastewater. Stripping is normally accomplished using air or steam, which increases volatility.

Adsorption of organic chemicals out of wastewater, involves the use of highly porous solids such as activated carbon, activated alumina, silica gel or resins, the surface of which will adsorb compatible organic compounds.

Ion exchange is a process which uses a bed of a resin to exchange unwanted anions for cations or visa versa.

Incineration is a rapid oxidation, or burning process in which organics are burned into carbon dioxide and water at temperatures in the range of 1000 to 1500oF.

As in the case of physical treatment, many types of chemical treatment are concentration methods which leave a much smaller *residual* which must be recycled or disposed of in a landfill.

Biological Treatment of Wastewater

The purpose of biological wastewater treatment is to use bacteria, instead of chemicals, to convert the dissolved organic hydrocarbon portion of the wastewater to CO_2 and water and to convert soluble organics into insoluble bacteria. Once insoluble, these solids can be physically settled or filtered to separate the clean water from the sludge residuals.

Wastewater may contain non- organic constituents in the form of inorganics such as metals and anionic compounds such as ammonia, nitrogen, phosphorous and sulfur compounds, halogens, non metals, salts, acids, bases and many other chemicals. Since biological wastewater treatment only breaks down hydrocarbons, these other compounds may need to be removed before or after the biological treatment.

The biological characterization of wastewater is a measure of the parameters which can affect the biological treatment. The biological strength can be estimated in 3 ways; by the measurement of the oxygen used in 5 days by a wastewater sample seeded with bacteria (Biochemical Oxygen Demand, BOD_5), by a measurement of the amount of potassium dichromate needed for complete oxidation (Chemical Oxygen Demand, COD), and by the measurement of the Total Organic Carbon (TOC) in the wastewater.

A test for one of the most common bacterial species, coliform bacteria, is normally required in a discharge permit. Other necessary tests include temperature, pH, nitrogen, phosphorous, ammonia and heavy metals.

Biological treatment can work in the presence of oxygen (aerobic treatment), or without the presence of oxygen (anaerobic treatment). The bacteria present in the process can be suspended in a basin (suspended growth), or attached to inert solid surfaces such as stones or plastic shapes (attached growth). The basins in which controlled bacterial activity occur can be concrete, metal, plastic or fiberglass structures or can be dirt ponds.

The size of these basins can vary from a 1000 gallon home septic tank to a multi million gallon municipal or industrial treatment system.

As in the case of physical and chemical wastewater treatment, biological treatment leaves a solid sediment after settling that must be recycled or disposed of through land disposal or some other acceptable method.

In addition to the direct discharge of wastewater, stormwater can contain or erode soil and wash pollutants into a receiving steam. This pollution can be minimized at its source by erosion prevention, screening, settling and/or filtering the runoff.

Our Challenge to Clean up the Land

The purpose of land pollution control is to, through science and engineering, clean and return soil to its natural state. As expressed above, land or soil and its vegetation is a receptor for pollutant discharges from society. Vegetation, depending on its extent and its characteristics, can uptake liquids through transpiration.

When soil is polluted beyond its allowable capacity, the only practical control for inorganics is to excavate, rinse and replace the soil, resulting in a liquid residual.

Organic pollutants, dissolved in groundwater can be removed from underground by pumping and treating the contaminated water on the surface. Several in situ (in place) bioremediation methods have been developed to destroy organic pollutants. These treatments have worked biologically using both aerobic and anaerobic treatment. The reason for this success is that the organic pollutants typically exist in water surrounding, or adsorbed within the soil particles. The treatment is therefore similar to the biological wastewater treatment described above.

Chapter 9

Our Stewardship of the Environment

Will I be a Christian Environmentalist?

As in any serious question we discuss with others or ask ourselves, we must understand the terms being discussed, but we also must understand the basis upon which we determine our answers.

In the context of the question asked in this book, we must face the relationships affected by the Fall, as listed in Chapter 7, between God, man and nature, and decide on the relative importance of each. If we do that objectively, we realize that normally in our thoughts, and even in the title of this book, the most important relationship is not considered; that between us and God.

God's relationship to us is not within our control. He is in charge of that relationship as Lord and Master and Sovereign God. Our position is really limited to believing in Him, loving Him, determining what He wants us to do, and doing it.

So, in order to answer the question posed in this book, we must determine our basis for making decisions. As discussed previously, if we realize that in order for matter to be created (in scientific language) from anything (non-matter, anti- matter, intelligence, imagination, etc.), a spiritual entity must be involved to transfer matter from the supernatural state to the natural state (the belief that certain matter *always existed*, is scientifically insufficient as an explanation).

Therefore, assuming a spiritual Creator, that Creator God must be omniscient or He would not be God. In His omniscience, only He can know completely what our relation to the environment should be. In effect, the entire scientific effort of mankind throughout history, only has a realistic goal of discovering God's plan for the environment. Our interest then, should be to discern God's will through a serious study of His Word as we make decisions relating to the environment.

As managers of the environment with dominion over it, our job, as decreed by God must be to glorify God and enjoy Him forever. One way to perform that chief end of man is to protect the environment for future generations, allowing sustainable growth. Our effort should result in retaining the general condition of the environment as it was created by God. God loved the environment as it was created. He said it was good!

Preserving our Body and our Mind

The first way we as individuals can preserve the environment, is to care for our most intimate part of the environment, our body and our mind. In Chapter 3 we discussed the Biblical relationship between our body and our mind and concluded that they were integrally related in Creation.

In Chapter 6, we studied some of the verses which refer to our responsibility toward our body and our mind. Romans 12:1b-2 tells us to: *present your bodies as a living sacrifice, holy and acceptable to God, which is your spiritual worship. Do not be conformed to this world, but be transformed by the renewal of your mind, that by testing you may discern what is the will of God, what is good and acceptable and perfect*. Our bodies and our minds, as God's temple should remain preserved as God created them, just as the rest of nature should, and not transformed into something we consider better than God could have done. In John 2:21-22 concerning Jesus' prophesy of raising the destroyed temple, John writes: *But* He *was speaking about the temple of* His *body, when therefore* He *was raised from the dead,* His *disciples remembered that* He *had said this, and they believed the scripture and the word that Jesus had spoken*. Jesus' body was also God's temple, as it was perfect even with the injuries from His murder, just as God created our bodies as a perfect temple in His sight.

The preservation of our body as God's temple, made in the image of God, should be one of our very highest priorities. Jesus sanctified our body when He took on human flesh and transfigured it, making it the temple of the Holy Spirit. It is obvious then, that we must preserve our body and our mind as God created them, and not believe that we can improve His work when we puncture, cut or tattoo our bodies as if we were improving God's image. I am not speaking of corrective medicine, practices or surgery. Leviticus 19:28 says: *You shall not make any cuts on your body for the dead or tattoo yourselves: I am the Lord*. We can rationalize that Jesus did away with the Levitical Laws, but contextually, the Levitical moral laws are permanent, the civil laws have been abrogated, except that the principles still apply, and only the ceremonial laws are done away with by Jesus' sacrifice.

Our minds can likewise be profaned (we may think *improved*) by mind altering drugs, and our bodies indulged and destroyed by the use of tobacco, over eating and under exercising. Our bodies and minds are probably the easiest part of the environment to protect, and yet we continue to abuse God's temple, destroying not only it, but our credibility as a witness of God.

A sad misrepresentation of God's Word by some Christians is to feel a freedom to use damaging and dangerous natural or synthetic products of God's creation to demonstrate that we are spiritually above and unconcerned with something as worldly as our bodies or minds, or to be a part of the world in order to attract or witness to the unsaved

(I Corinthians 6:12: *All things are lawful for me, but not all things are helpful. All things are lawful for me, but I will not be enslaved by anything.* See also I Corinthians 10:23.)

There is no mandate from God for us to not use and enjoy the environment for our sustenance. God allows us to kill vegetation and animals for food, clothing and shelter.

His specific directions for the tabernacle and the temple even included vegetation and animal products. So the key to sustainable growth seems to be the use and replacement of renewable resources, and the prudent use and substitution for non-renewable resources.

Available Natural Resources

Our natural resources originate from the same three realms of the environment which we have been discussing; air, water and land.

Air Resources

The unpolluted air consists of gases that can be used for sustainable growth. The volume of the atmosphere is so great compared to the need for these gases by civilization, that there is currently no need for replacement. Therefore our responsibility is to return the mixture of these gases as God created them.

To date, the only gas that has become unbalanced is carbon dioxide (CO_2). CO_2 has increased from about 260 ppm in 800 AD to 360 ppm in 2000 AD

(1). This is a possibility for environmental regulatory efforts and is discussed in Chapters 4 and 8.

Water Resources

Water is a large source of natural resources, providing aquatic life for food, salt for seasoning and potentially other salts and minerals. Much of the inorganic content of the water apparently has been present since Creation, because aquatic life has been in the water since the fifth day of Creation, and aquatic life requires inorganic nutrients to survive. In addition, many of the minerals in the waters of the earth originated in the soil of the earth, and were eroded and washed through streams and rivers to the ocean, the final sink.

Land Resources

The largest amount of resources used by humans is from the land. There are two basic types of these resources below the surface of the ground; organic and inorganic. Once these resources are removed, it is virtually impossible to replace them at the source. Organics have their source from fossils and include peat, oil, gas, coal and diamonds; the result of pressurizing organic matter over time. Except for diamonds, these resources should be considered as

---

(1) *Do the planets and the Sun Control our Climate and the CO2 in the Atmosphere?*, Fred Goldberg, International Conference on Climate Change, 2009, New York, NY.

not only non-replaceable, but as adding carbon to the atmosphere when converted into energy by burning.

As consumers of energy, we directly add CO_2, methane, oxides of nitrogen and sulfur oxides to the atmosphere when we burn these materials in our automobiles, heaters, stoves, ovens and water heaters. We likewise, contribute to the addition of these materials to the atmospheric carbon cycle when we use electricity, buy products which are manufactured and transported, or use public transportation.

There are three types of land resources on the surface of the land; vegetation, soil and surface minerals. These resources, especially vegetation, are generally replaceable and do not add to the carbon cycle over time.

The Residuals of Civilization

With the passage of time, certain residuals of civilization remain and re-enter the environment through the air, the water or the land.

Natural Residuals

Even without the existence of humans, vegetable and animal life produces a large amount of waste through death and decay, animal excrement, forest fires, volcanoes, earthquakes, tsunamis, etc. A small amount of these residuals end up in the air. The residuals entering the soil are mostly recycled, but the runoff of residuals to bodies of water can cause around 25 percent of water pollution.

Natural decay has been estimated to release over eight times as much CO_2 to the atmosphere as the amount emitted by humans (1).

Agricultural Residuals

Like natural residuals, agricultural residuals are minimal additions into the air and soil, but can add another approximate 25 percent of the total water pollution through runoff of soil, fertilizer, herbicides and pesticides.

Municipal Residuals

Municipalities voluntarily collect and dispose of certain residuals including sewage, landfill leachate (underground leaking into the soil), burned trash and garbage, and stormwater runoff. All of these residual disposals are highly regulated by the EPA and have improved our air, water and soil quality since the 1960's, but there are still large amounts of these residuals entering our environment.

Industrial Residuals

Industrial air emissions, water discharges and solid waste disposal are regulated by the EPA, as explained in Chapters 4 and 8 of this book. Regulatory improvements continue to be made, but sadly, certain environmental groups have slowed this process by

---

(1) *U.S. Global Change Research Information Office, Common Questions about Climate Change*

filing lawsuits that tend to delay promulgated EPA Rules and Regulations.

Municipal and industrial residuals make up the remaining 50 percent of water pollution.

The U.S. Greenhouse Gas Emissions Inventory estimated that in 2006, fossil fuel combustion accounted for 94% of all human sources of CO_2 emissions, 2% was from non-energy use of fuels, and the rest was from industrial manufacturing and production.

Of the fossil fuel combustion, approximately 43% was from electricity production (83% of that from coal), 32% from transportation, 15.6% from industrial, 5% from residential, 3.5% from commercial and 0.9% from U.S. Territories. CO_2 was 84.8% of all human caused emissions.

Personal Residuals

Our personal and family choices have a large effect on the environment. Our personal transportation uses require energy, discharge pollutants and may end up as solid wastes when abandoned. The current interest in electric transportation may not be an answer because of the life cycle costs of producing and operating these vehicles, such as battery and vehicle manufacturing, and battery recharges using fossil fuel energy.

Our heat for water and homes is provided directly or indirectly by hydraulic, nuclear, fossil fuel and to a very minor extent, alternative energy.

We discharge our wastewater from urine, feces, garbage disposal, dish washing and clothes washing into the ground through septic tanks or to municipal sewage treatment plants. Note that the purpose of the "water" in wastewater is simply to transport the waste to a point of treatment and then discharge it to a body of water.

Since soil biodegrades organics, stores inorganics, and uses water for transpiration of vegetation, if we were able to transfer all of our urine, feces, garbage, dish washing liquid and clothes washing liquid into the ground, our municipal sewage treatment plants would be unnecessary.

Personally, our garbage (food wastes) and trash is disposed of privately or publicly through dumps, landfills or incinerators.

What We Can Do

All of these residuals of civilization are discharged to the air, the water or to the land after transportation and treatment under regulatory supervision of the EPA. Many of our personal choices can affect the weight and volume of these residuals which enter the environment.

A suggestion for each of us, as individuals or as part of industry, commerce or government, is to examine the extent of the residuals that we can control in terms of pounds per year. Then we can determine if, and how these residuals re-enter the environment.

Residuals Accounting

The State of California has for decades, followed an environmental policy to require industries to examine their total waste discharge and to commit to its annual reduction. This policy requires the industry to justify that the raw materials it purchases cause the minimal environmental pollution. In addition, it requires a critical look for the same purpose at whether these materials can be substituted for less polluting materials. They must also analyze their manufacturing process for minimizing pollution, and even to see if the final disposal of their products can produce less waste.

This philosophy can be used for us, as individuals in our effort to be stewards of God's gifts. I would recommend the study and possible adoption of a process similar to one developed for greenhouse gas emissions called *The GHG Protocol for Project Accounting* which offers an objective approach to accounting for residual discharges of all types. This Protocol was published by The World Resources Institute of the United States and The World Business Council for Sustainable Development of Geneva, Switzerland. This group is a coalition of around 200 industries, governments and non-government organizations launched in 1998 to develop internationally accepted greenhouse gas (ghg) accounting and reporting standards.

The following is a recommendation for using these principles for anyone desiring to be an environmental steward:

1. Write a *Missions Statement* expressing in a sentence or paragraph form, the purpose of your residuals reduction effort.
2. Determine the boundaries of your plan for direct uses.
3. Estimate the pounds per year of waste discharged under your control for direct and indirect uses and the base discharge amount for comparison.
4. Determine discharge lowering goals.
5. Document the intended method of residuals reduction, the amount per year of reduction, and the ultimate goal.

The Mission Statement

The Mission Statement should be a simple expression of what you are going to do, agreed to by all involved parties. A possible statement could be: *The goal of this plan is to follow Biblical principles in assuring that we lower the total amount of residuals under our control which are returned to the environment.* Since this statement is the first step of the accounting process, the amount and timing of the reductions has not been set.

Plan Boundaries

The boundaries of your plan are two fold; the geographical boundary and the organizational boundary.

Geographical Boundary

The geographical boundary is the physical area from which discharges to the environment occur. This, from a family or individual standpoint, can be your property, or a portion of your property, whether owned, rented or leased.

Organizational Boundary

The second, and overlapping boundary which should be considered is the organizational boundary. This boundary includes the environmental discharges from products and systems which you own or control. Controlled products or systems could be rented, leased or sub-contracted. They could include transportation off site for errands, deliveries, etc. Discharges from these products or systems can be included or excluded from accounting, but should be clearly understood when comparing results.

Life Cycle Analysis

The geographical and/or the organizational boundary could literally be the world, if you complete your accounting on a life cycle basis. The philosophy of a life cycle analysis is that the environmental "footprint" or discharge of every organic or inorganic product or system used is considered a residual or waste. The life cycle analysis can be limited to the direct uses controlled, or can include indirect discharges associated with the product or system. This is true, whether the product or system is energy, fuel, food, durable goods or expendable goods.

The environmental footprint is that of a product or system from "cradle to grave". This means that the air, water and land discharges during the manufacture, distribution, storage, delivery, disposal, etc. of a product are included in the accounting.

Products or systems, once received or initiated, may have an environmental footprint during the life of their use.

At some point, the product or system may have served its purpose, or be used up. For instance, energy, during its use has an environmental footprint, but once used, has no footprint, other than ash from some fossil fuels such as wood, peat or coal if the product is burned, or leachate, if it is stored in a landfill.

Most practitioners of residuals accounting do not use a life cycle analysis, since theoretically, each supplier, transporter, user, etc. is responsible for his own accounting, and if everyone practiced life cycle analyses, there would be a huge overlapping of reporting.

Estimating Residual Discharges

Residual discharges may be direct or indirect. Direct discharges are those which are released to the air, the water or the land either directly from their source, or through a private or public service.

Examples of direct source discharges are all air emissions including escaping smoke or vapors from fuels, water discharges through septic tanks, and on property trash, composting or garbage dumps.

Re-use of residuals would normally be complete (gifts, sales, etc.), but recycling could be only partial. For instance, a scrap iron recycling company typically sends the cloth, leather and possibly the plastic to a landfill, while recycling only the metals.

Examples of indirect discharges are sewerage systems and trash/garbage pick up or hauling to private or public systems.

Calculations for Direct Discharges

Direct discharges can be estimated as follows:

1. Coal: 5408 pounds CO_2 per ton coal plus:
   12 pounds of oxides of nitrogen (NOx) plus:
   67 pounds of sulfur dioxide (SO_2) plus:
   71 pounds of Particulate Matter (PM) (1)
2. Natural Gas: 95.94 pounds of CO_2 per 1000 cubic feet of gas (1)
3. Fuel Oil: 18.86 pounds of CO_2 per gallon of oil (1)
4. Wood: 5700 pounds CO_2 per ton of wood plus 40 pounds PM per ton of wood (2)
5. Septic tank discharges can be estimated at 0.20 pounds of solids per day per person which will eventually need to be hauled unless it is organic and biologically degraded.

---

(1) Fuel Oil Calculator, USDA, Forestry Product Laboratory, *Natural Gas and the Environment*", natural gas.org

(2) *Air Pollution from Wood Burning Fireplaces and Stoves*, Toronto Public Health Department, and The Engineering Tool Box, *Combustion Fuels CO2 Emissions*

6. Trash and garbage disposal on site can be estimated in pounds per day as land pollution.

Calculations for Indirect Discharges

Indirect, or off site discharges can be estimated as follows:

1. Sewerage system discharges can be estimated at 0.20 pounds of solids per day plus 100 gallons of water per person per day. The weight of the solids in the sewage contains the constituents that can harm the environment. The liquid, which is virtually all water, is returned as relatively pure water to the stream downstream from where it was taken.
2. Trash and garbage disposal off site can be estimated in pounds per day.
3. Durable goods disposed of should be considered trash unless they are recycled or re-used by others.

Estimating Transportation Discharges

Automobile emissions have been estimated by the EPA (1) as follows:

Pollutant	Cars, pounds/mile	Light Truck, pounds/mile
Total Hydrocarbons	0.006167	0.007731
Carbon Monoxide	0.046035	0.061013
Oxides of Nitrogen	0.003061	0.003987
Carbon Dioxide	0.916	1.15

Large Trucks

The emissions from large trucks vary from those of light trucks to about four times those rates.

Public Transportation

The following are recommendations for CO_2 emissions from public transportation:

Source	Pounds/mile	Description
Private Auto	0.96	1.58 passengers average
Bus	0.64	28% Full

---

(1) *Emissions Facts; Average Annual Emissions and Fuel Consumption for passenger cars and Light trucks*, (August 14, 2007)

Heavy Rail	0.22	Rapid transit; inter city, 47% Full
Light Rail	0.36	Electric street cars; trams, 37% Full
Commuter Rail	0.33	30% Full
Van Pool	0.22	56% Full

These are average emissions estimates from *Public Transportation's Role in Responding to Climate Change*, U.S. Department of Transportation, Federal Transit Administration

Other Discharges

Individuals may discharge other residuals or have power uses not listed above which will add to the total annual environmental footprint.

What Then?

If we are led by God's Word to do our part to be stewards of the environment, whether we go to the effort of accounting for our emissions and setting reduction goals, or whether we just do our best to protect the environment, we can, and should be a Christian environmentalist.

The accumulative effect of a significant pollutant discharge reduction by Christians world wide would benefit ourselves and those who come after us, but more importantly, it would demonstrate our obedience to God. There would be less need for what some see as unfair environmental regulations if Christians would be proper stewards of what God gave us. Indeed, if Christians would follow Biblical principles in all areas of public concern, the necessity of government regulation, often necessarily unequal or unfair, would be greatly minimized.

When we study God's Word carefully, God is not necessarily *fair* from our perspective. But he is absolutely just and right and true. If He were *fair* to all people in their judgment, there would be compromise and not justice. Many demand fairness in order to gain something, even if their position is completely wrong and unjust from a Biblical prospective. If we, as Christians, were to seek God's truth in all things, rather than our good, comfort and prosperity, we could live on a higher plane with our efforts devoted vertically to God, and outwardly to others and the environment, instead of inwardly.

Practical Examples

The following are several examples of how we as individuals can aid directly or indirectly in our responsibility as stewards of the environment:

1. Support efforts such as the Comprehensive Everglades Restoration Plan, a program managed to restore the natural stormwater distribution.
2. Support privately granted Wilderness Preserves which deed tracts of land to a permanent trust which prohibits their use for anything other than the preservation of the natural state of the land.

3. Promote wildlife and forestry management to enable people to beneficially use their property without depleting its resources.
4. The management of invasive species of animals and vegetation can be locally accomplished by individuals or regionally accomplished by governments or organizations. Examples are the control of Kudzu, the beautiful but destructive lion fish, the python and tree blights.
5. The consideration of Christians who should love all of God's people, to allow the less fortunate or less trained equal opportunity to enjoy the aesthetic pleasures of God's Creation, whether on private or public property, while balancing access with survival of the environment.
6. Unselfish sharing of our property, neighborhoods and towns for relatively undesirable environmental related projects such as tree farms, windmills, solar farms, landfills, sewage treatment plants, etc. Should we *tithe* our land resources for the benefit of others as Christians?

The old NIMBY (not in my backyard) argument does not seem to be of concern to God who owns all of our property anyway. We have spaces in our houses like bathrooms, trash areas and laundry rooms, which are not exactly pleasant areas to hang out, but we can close them off. Can't we do the same thing with our community land instead of whining *NIMBY*?

Why is it Important?

As far as our relation to the environment is concerned, we can be educated as to the need, but what is education other than learning the knowledge or beliefs of someone else? For instance, philosophy is basically the study of the writings of philosophers, rather than a study of how to think and develop new thoughts. Every teacher, every scientist, every theologian and every writer has a bias which affects their beliefs and their communication. So, when we learn about the environment, the only reliable reference is the Bible, as written by the One who created the environment, and has no bias, other than the truth, in His communication.

Moses warned us in Deuteronomy 4:2 and 12:32 that: *You shall not add to the* Word *that I command you, nor take away from it, that you may keep the commandments of the Lord your God that I command you*, and Deuteronomy 12:32 that: *Everything that I command you, you shall be careful to do. You shall not add to it or take from it.* Solomon, in Proverbs 30: 5-6, says: *Every word of God proves true; he is a shield to those who take refuge in him. Do not add to his words, lest he rebuke you and you be found a liar.* John, in Revelation 22: 18-19 says: *I warn everyone who hears the words of the prophesy of this book: if anyone adds to them, God will add to him the plagues described in this book, and if anyone takes away from the words of the book of this prophesy, God will take away his share in the tree of life and the holy city, which are described in this book..*

All of our efforts toward better understanding our relation to our environment are futile unless they are grounded in the Bible and do not add to or take away from its words.

Why we are Here

In summary, the Bible tells us that the triune God; the Father, the Son and the Holy Spirit has existed and will exist throughout eternity. From this supernatural spiritual existence, God created for the first time a natural, physical inorganic earth surrounded by water with day and night, but no sun or universe (Genesis 1:1-5), the next day God created the inorganic sky (Genesis 1: 6-8); then on the third day, God separated the waters and the dry land and presumably allowed the inorganics carbon dioxide and hydrogen to form organic plants, and for these organics to combine with inorganics to form DNA, RNA and protein, the essentials of life (Genesis 1:9-13).

On the fourth day, God created the rest of the inorganic universe for signs, seasons, days, years and light (Genesis 1: 14-19), then the fifth day of Creation saw the water and air creatures appear (Genesis 1: 20-23) with the necessary DNA arrangement to form living animals.

God created land animals on the sixth day and lastly, humans with their unique DNA in His likeness (Genesis 1: 24-31).

We know from the Bible that this effort to create the universe took God six days and His only *tool* was His Word.

A Christian Environmentalist

God's complete Creation was good and existed in harmony until Adam and Eve. The first humans were tempted by Satan to believe that they could *be like God* (Genesis 3:5). They yielded to this temptation, as we continue to do today, and were punished by banishment from the perfect existence with God in the Garden of Eden. We have inherited this curse today, since our tendency is to succumb to the same sin.

But God in His grace sent Jesus, His Son to live on earth, to communicate God's love for us, to defeat Death and the curse, and to explain His plan for us to spend a spiritual eternity with Him.

Jesus humbled Himself to abuse, torture and death as a sacrifice in order to pay the justifiable punishment for our sin of wanting to be God. Through the act of Jesus' death, resurrection and ascension back into the spiritual world He came from, our sins have been forgiven and as pure saints, our future death is assured to be followed by a spiritual ascension into Heaven to spend eternity with our Father, the triune God of our creation.

Meanwhile, God left us here to praise God, to enjoy Him and to accept His love, with a mandate to fill the earth, subdue it and have dominion over every living thing (Genesis 1: 28-30). This mandate answers the question in the title of this book. *Yes, we must be Christian environmentalists!* The term is not an oxymoron but a command from Almighty God to serve, respect and use the environment that He created with love, for His glory and our well being until the Day that Jesus returns and gives us the perfect environment which we can enjoy forever in His presence. ***Amen!***

About the Author

E. Roberts Alley is a registered Professional Engineer in 19 states and has practiced and taught environmental engineering for over 50 years, working primarily for industrial and municipal clients to lower their residual discharges to the environment.

Bob is Chairman of the Board of New Era Holdings, Inc. He has BE and MS degrees from Vanderbilt University and has taught environmental courses at Vanderbilt, the University of Tennessee, George Washington University, The Centre for Management Technology and several other universities and organizations, as well as in England, France, Singapore, Malaysia and Indonesia.

He has been an Elder in two Presbyterian churches and a Deacon in another and has taught youth and adult Sunday School for 30 years. Bob was a Scoutmaster for 20 years and has 4 children and 9 grandchildren.

He lives in Nashville, Tennessee and Long Key Florida.

Books by E. Roberts Alley

Drainage Management, 1991, University of Tennessee Center for Government Training,
Air Quality Control Handbook, 1998, McGraw –Hill
Water Quality Control Handbook, 2000, McGraw Hill
Manual de Control de la Calidad del Aire, 2001, McGraw-Hill
Water Quality Control Handbook, Second Edition, 2007, McGraw-Hill

CPSIA information can be obtained at www.ICGtesting.com
Printed in the USA
LVOW080055050613

336905LV00001B/1/P